Workforce Summer

and

Job Success

(And Beyond)

WORKFORCE SUMMER JOB SUCCESS

(AND BEYOND)

By Edward DeJesus

First Printing, First Edition 2020

ISBN: 978-0-578-72435-5

DeJesus Solutions, LLC
www.edwarddejesus.com

CHAPTER 1

Let's keep it real… Having a job isn't going to stop you from being caught up in drugs or crime. It's not going to save you from making bad decisions. And it most definitely isn't going to change the mindset that you don't have a choice. The truth is, being a success won't come from the job you have. But it will come from the simple understanding that you are in control, that you have the ability to **CHOOSE** to be alive and free.

To be truly alive and free starts as a declaration. As a statement that becomes a matter of fact. You have to know it and you have to **OWN IT**.

So, when I say, "Alive and Free," I want you to shout, "Free and Alive." (And actually say it aloud.)

Alive and Free!

Free and alive!

Really shout it out!

Alive and Free!

Free and Alive!

Alive and Free!

Free and Alive!

That's right. You are free and alive, and this book is going to guide you through taking the necessary steps toward making the most out of your life and taking advantage of your freedom.

While we will be discussing workplace success, understand that this book **is not about a job (**Although we will teach you the skills, strategies and techniques that you will need to make sure that you get a job and never have to look for another job again).

This book is about advancing your life, freedom, and future economic opportunity. It's about becoming a better version of yourself. About moving past the doubts and discouragement placed upon you by society. It's about shutting up all of the naysayers who said "you can't" or "you'll fail" and instead, securing that financial future and making enough money to keep you comfortable and happy.

I want you to think about this for a moment:

How many people do you know who have a job but are still broke?

How many people do you know who have a job but are still hooked on drugs?

How many people do you know who have a job but still wind up in jail?

The truth is you can have a job and still spend your paycheck on things that endanger your life and your freedom. You can have a job and the only thing you get out of it is a terrible record of attendance and punctuality.

This is why I am not here to help you get a job.

In fact, **you already have a job** - *staying alive, free, and building your future economic opportunity* – that's your job! I am here to help you do your job, while also showing you how to build a career and achieve a level of economic prosperity that you may have never dreamed possible.

Let's take a minute to walk through a simple exercise. I want you to think about:

- Why you are here
- What you want to accomplish

Take a minute to answer the following questions.

Why are you here? In other words, what made you pick up this book and begin the path to success?

_____

_____

_____

What do you want to accomplish? What do you hope to achieve by using this guide?

_____

_____

_____

Here are some answers that we received from hundreds of young people:

- ❖ To get a job, to earn some money
- ❖ To make a better future
- ❖ To get work experience
- ❖ To stay off the streets
- ❖ To have something to do
- ❖ Because of my mom

One thing that all of these answers have in common is a **_positive goal_**.

A "job" is a tool to help you build the skills, abilities, and behaviors that will help you become a productive and successful person. As we said earlier, **it's just a way to help you do your real job!**

We all have jobs, or roles, in our lives. My role is father, brother, husband, youth advocate, and triathlete. Having a job is a major factor in helping me to do my job. It allows me to put food on the table, support my family, invest in helping young people, not to mention purchase equipment so I can race triathlons. _If I don't have a role; If I don't see myself as something, I can't do my job!_

There are two types of forces that influence our self-concept or how we see our roles in life: internal forces and external forces.

Internal forces include what you think about yourself, the things you pay attention to, how you process life's events, and how you mentally deal with failure and success.

External forces include your environment, the people you hang with, the labels that others put on you, and those that you put on yourself.

In a few minutes, you're going to go through an exercise where you will identify the internal and external forces that influence your self- concept. But first, I want to share a few things for you to keep in mind as you are going through the exercise.

Internal and external forces can be positive or negative.

When negative forces affect your self-concept, it is never too late to begin taking positive steps to improve the way you think. You can do this by changing the way you view different situations, switching up your self-talk, and adjusting your belief systems.

In the next section, you will look at an external and internal force and rank their influence on your self-concept using the **MAKiN' iT Survival Scale**.

What is the Survival Scale, you ask?

The Survival Scale is a decision-making tool that we created to help people reflect on where they are going in life and the forces that are supporting or stopping them in the process.

It looks a little something like this...

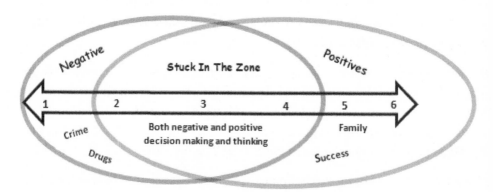

This scale represents the internal and external forces in your life that either push you toward true survival (going up the scale) or pushes you away from true survival (going down the scale).

The key is to reflect on a particular force in your life and give it a number.

If that force is damaging and **completely negative** like dealing with drugs, facing or dealing with incarceration, or dealing with violence, rank that force as a **1**.

Why? Because it is clearly pushing you *AWAY* from true survival.

2, 3, and 4 rankings represent certain forces that have a **blend of negative and positive forces**.

For example, maybe you're on a sports team (which is good) but it's causing your grades to slip (not so good.) Or maybe there is a person in your life that you consider a good influence or mentor, yet they abuse drugs. These forces can keep you "stuck in the zone" and can make it difficult for you to move forward.

5 and 6 rankings are what we consider to be **completely positive**. These are forces that push you toward true survival and a positive future. This can be your family members, getting good grades in school, or killin' it at work.

I want you to give this a go and use the scale to rank an external and internal force.

For example, I would list my Triathlons as an external force and give it a 5.3 on the scale. Triathlons are incredibly positive, but I do spend a lot of time training and this cuts into time with family. On my internal list, I would rate my anxiety a 3.4, although it can throw me into a sense of discomfort, it does keep me alert and on my toes.

Your turn!

	External	Internal
Force		
Rank		
Reason for Rank		

Handling External and Internal Influences

Now that you identified the forces that are endangering your life, freedom, and future economic opportunity, it's time to think about ways of handling them.

****Spoiler Alert: this step can be pretty challenging****

Often people don't want to admit that they are enrolled in the "*Unemployment Training System*." I call it UTS; a school and mindset that trains people to be chronically unemployed or underemployed.

Do you know someone who goes there?

It's a place where people do things that don't promote their life, freedom, and future economic opportunity, yet they do them anyway. Why?

I wish it were a simple answer.

Greed, power, discrimination, and inadequate support and education are all major reasons why the UTS was founded. Yet, none of that matters because we don't want to go anywhere near it. Tuition is free and they try to enroll you through an overload of bad information, bad advice, bad examples, and bad instruction.

Believe me when I tell you, I was enrolled in UTS for a hot minute. It's a nasty place full of viruses. Here are some of the viruses that got me sick:

- ➤ Fake friends telling me "it's not illegal if we don't get caught."

- ➤ People trying to convince me that skipping school is a good investment.

- ➤ Older kids who tried to convince me that it's better to be caught with it than without it.

- ➤ Drug dealers who tried to make the case that I could make more money in a day than my teacher made all week.

I got so sick I had to drop out. And thank God I did. I enrolled in the **Workforce Development System** and never looked back.

All of that was normal where I grew up and unfortunately, to this day, it is still normal in many of the communities where I work. But the good news is that there was, and still are, many positive forces that act like vaccines against these UTS viruses by telling us:

- ➤ A true friend will never lead you to danger.

- ➤ Education has the biggest payoff.

- ➤ It's okay to fail, just get up and try again.

- ➤ Walk away and live another day.

It's up to you whether you WANT to enroll in the Unemployment Training System or the Workforce Development System. If you let the negative influences go unchecked, guess which one you'll graduate from?

Now it's time to train you to maximize the positive influences and minimize the negative. I don't want you to get caught up out there. I'll walk you through a plan that'll bring on the positives and ditch the negatives.

First, I want you to think about the positive messages you receive and how you process them.

Positive messages are everywhere. They can come from parents or guardians, mentors, teachers, friends, community leaders, family members, neighbors, and even celebrities. Try to think of a specific *positive* message that was shared with you.

What was it?

_____

_____

_____

Who gave it?

_____

_____

_____

What made it so great?

_____

_____

_____

Let me give you an example of my own.

I sometimes hear that I am an awesome swimmer.

My triathlete buddies often tell me this.

What makes it so great is that I feel recognized for all the hard work that I put into learning how to swim after 40.

Now think back to the *negative* information that you received.

What was it?

_____

_____

_____

Who gave it?

_____

_____

_____

What made it so bad?

_____

_____

_____

Let me give you another example.

I often hear that there is something wrong with me.

It's anxiety knocking at the door.

What makes it so bad is that there is nothing wrong with me. It just makes me scared.

It's good to be aware of the positive and negative messages and influences in our lives. But knowing how to use them to our advantage is just as important. That's what we'll take a look at in the next chapter.

Using the Power of Reinforcement and Reframing for Success

Ain't no shame in embracing a positive message or moment.

We all love to be told when we're doing good and being recognized for our talents. When we receive these positive messages, we're often taught to just smile and say, "Thank you." But what if we could take those messages and transform them into real tools for success? That's what we're going to do.

We're going to practice reinforcing the good information and challenging the negative. This is how we will do it….

For every good example and advice that you received, I want you to respond with the phrase: *What I heard you say is….* And complete the sentence by ***positively reinforcing the message – taking it to another level.***

For example, if someone told me: *"Ed, you have so much potential."*

I'll respond: *"What I heard you say is **that I am a leader and I'm in charge of my life.**"*

For every negative example and advice that you received, you will respond with the same phrase: *What I heard you say is….*but this time you will complete the sentence by ***flipping (reframing) the message back on the person who sent it.***

For example, if someone told me: *"Ed, let's cut class and smoke a blunt."*

I'll respond: *"What I heard you say is **that you don't value education and you don't value your future.**"*

Now you try. Think of one positive and one negative message that you received recently. Using what you just learned, on the next page describe and reframe these messages.

What was the POSITIVE message you received?

_____

_____

Now, reinforce it.

What I heard you say was...

_____

_____

What was the NEGATIVE message you received?

_____

_____

Now, reframe it.

What I heard you say was...

_____

_____

Reinforcing and **Reframing** are powerful skills that will help you develop a different way of looking at a situation, a person, or a relationship by changing or supporting its meaning.

They will be important assets to help you develop your workforce success mindset.

Fixed and Growth Mindsets

As you learned in the last exercise, there are forces that influence how we see our roles in life. If we let negative forces influence us, we may have a **negative, or fixed, mindset.** If we let positive things influence us, we will have a **positive or growth mindset.**

Many people have a fixed mindset towards things that they find overwhelming or challenging. A fixed mindset sees things as unchangeable. In a fixed mindset, people don't see room for growth and development. Learning becomes too hard and, therefore, change is often never made. In a fixed mindset, people say things like *"This is too hard,"* or *"I'm so stupid."* To give you an example, let's say you work at a grocery store. Your job is usually to stock shelves, but today your supervisor asked you to work the cash register. You've only had a couple of days of training, but your supervisors assure you that you've got this. A person with a fixed mindset would try to convince the supervisor to choose someone else to work the register. They'll whole-heartedly believe they are not ready to take on the task and will somehow mess things up.

A growth mindset, on the other hand, will help you overcome these doubts. A growth mindset is characterized by a willingness to confront challenges. It is characterized by the belief that one's intelligence and abilities can be improved with effort and the right strategies. People with a growth mindset say things like "I'll find a way to improve," or I'm not there yet." If you were working in the grocery store with a growth mindset, you would take on the challenge of working the register and see it as an opportunity to put your training to good use and a chance to improve. We all can train our brains to operate in a growth mindset framework.

Can you think of a time when you had a growth mindset?

_____

_____

_____

_____

How about when you had a fixed mindset?

_____

_____

_____

_____

ROLES

Your roles in life are greatly influenced by a fixed or growth mindset. Having a growth mindset will help you succeed in all of your roles. Now, let's look at your roles in life and what you want to get out of them. We'll start by doing an exercise that will define your current roles.

Keep in mind, your roles can reflect who you are (i.e. friend, brother, sister) or what you do (i.e. manager, supervisor, employee.)

Step 1: List up to 5 roles in your life: ****It's alright if it's less than 5****

     Role 1 _____

     Role 2 _____

     Role 3 _____

     Role 4 _____

     Role 5 _____

Step 2: List ways that a job could support you in that role:

     Role 1

_____

_____

Role 2

_____

_____

Role 3

_____

_____

Role 4

_____

_____

Role 5

_____

_____

Step three: Identify a success point in that role.

For example, if your role is a student, the success point might be graduation. Write down how you will feel when you graduate.

	Role	Success Point	How You'll Feel When You Reach That Point
1			
2			

3		
4		
5		

It's important to remember that **your role will change throughout your life.** As you're thinking about roles, please understand that what's important to you now may not be important to you eight years from now.

In fact, it's worth revisiting this exercise regularly, especially every time you face a major life decision. Because we always need to be clear on our roles at any given point in our lives.

Before we go any further, I want to let you know that I recognize the moves you have already made in your advancement toward freedom and success.

Here's what I know.

I know that you had to get up in the morning and get dressed.

You had to find information about the program.

You had to get the consent of a parent or guardian.

You had to get your working papers and fill out an application.

You had to get **HERE**.

You are making moves. But you may not often be recognized for the moves you make. So, let me be the first to say congratulations.

In the next section, you will have the chance to list the moves that you had to make to get here and I don't want you to leave anything out.

The Feeling of Success: Part 1

To be a success you need to know that you are worth it. Let's do a little exercise.

Let's pretend that I can't see you, but you can see me.

When you see Ed, what do you see? Say three positive things about me.

Keep them coming...

I feel it. That felt good...

Are you serious?

Ahhhh, Thank you.

That's it?

What, I look like Obama?

In fact, hop on social media right now and send those good things to me using *#ededucates*.

Now your turn. You're going to write down three *positive* things about yourself.

Ready? Complete the sentence:

> **When I see me , I see**

> _____

When I see me , I see

_____

When I see me , I see

_____

Now let's add how you feel when you hear those positive things.

When I hear that, I feel

_____

When I hear that, I feel

_____

When I hear that, I feel

_____

Often, we are not used to hearing positive things about ourselves. And, we often don't practice reinforcing the positive things that we do hear.

Earlier we learned about the power of reinforcement.

Try this activity every day in the morning and at night. Be loving and kind to yourself every time, no matter the situation. Remember, how you start the day will control how you end it.

The Feeling of Success: Part 2

What did you write down? Here is what I know.

You are beautiful?

You are caring?

You speak the truth?

You want respect?

You care for others sometimes more than you care for yourself?

You love your family?

You have a great smile?

You are smart. You are funny?

You have more potential than most people can understand?

You are talented?

How do I know? I've been doing this for thirty years and I have seen you before. I know you!!!! I know how bright you are, and I know the wonderful potential that you have.

You can set it off any way you choose!

It's up to you and this is the starting point.

You are defined by who you <u>think</u> you are.

So, you may have not been born with a silver spoon in your mouth, but here's what you got - a long history of people who took the worst and survived to be the best. You know something that others don't. You know you can "Make it!"

You know it takes more than dope lyrics and a good jump shot. It takes discipline, patience, hard work, and a determined focus.

You are a Dancer, a Rapper, and a Skater. You are a Gamer, a Rocker, an Athlete, and a Goth. You are committed, dedicated, and in it for life. **You are America's invisible front-line warriors.** Young people, not bonded together based on color, but on **<u>struggle</u>**. And you know that, in a struggle, you're supposed to sweat.

You don't need a Benz or a Lex to define you. You can pump a 12-speed and still represent more pride and integrity than most people can comprehend. **You overcome it. You do without it. You get by it. You get over it. You go around it. You duck under it. <u>You get it done!</u>**

Your numbers are in the millions. And, you want you to be a part of a family. A family with street-side smarts and boardroom potential. A family that knows that **a hustle is not a job**; that **a job is not a career**, and **a career is definitely not a calling**. You got the answer: If others can do it, you can, too.

As I said, you can set it off any way you choose. It's up to you and this is the starting point! Look in the mirror and say "I like me" I got this! I can't be stopped. I won't be stopped. Summer Job Success is mine! I'll get it done!

Download the MAKiN' iT Set-It Off pledge. It's our gift to you. If you are interested in being a part of the MAKiN' iT Nation' just sign the pledge, take a picture of it, and send it to us on Instagram at *www.makinitnation.com*.

Building Your Support Network: Part 1

You may have seen the title of this lesson and figured it would be about networking. Far from it!

Social capital building is not networking. Networking is an *activity*; social capital building is an *outcome*.

It's about getting people to care about helping you achieve your goals and you caring about helping others achieve theirs. We'll get more into the importance of it later but for now, let's get started on the social capital building process.

In this exercise, you will list three important people in your life whose contact information you possess. Add me as the fourth person. You can contact me at *@ededucates*. I also want you to write down two positive things about each person and then immediately email, text, or call the person with the simple message "I want to thank you for (fill in one positive thing about that person)".

Person 1: _____

Two positives about them:

_____

_____

Person 2: _____

Two positives about them:

_____

_____

Person 3: _____

Two positives about them:

_____

_____

Person 4: _____ *Ed DeJesus* _____

Two positives about them:

_____

_____

In the next lesson, we'll check to see if you're happy with the response.

Building Your Support Network: Part 2

So how did it go? Did you get a response? What did they say? Please share some of the responses...

Now, let's process that last exercise by answering a few questions.

How do you think you made that person feel?

_____

_____

_____

How does it feel to know that you made a person feel that way?

_____

_____

_____

What would you gain if you keep making people feel happy?

_____

_____

_____

That's it! That's the ticket to success. It's not what you know and it's not who you know. *It's who knows you and likes you* that is going to help you get a job and build a career. We call that **social capital.**

Most Americans get jobs through personal and family connections. It's the number one job search and success method. It beats putting in online applications and visiting employment agencies combined.

Think about it.

If the number one way to get a job is through personal and family connections, wouldn't we be fake if we didn't help you do what successful people do to get a job?

Could we really call ourselves the MAKiN' iT **Workforce and Summer Job Success** program?

Throughout this guide, you will be challenged to reach out to others, and we want you to do it. It is so important. We are also teaching your sponsoring agency how to build a social capital framework to support you in these efforts.

In the next lesson, we are going to focus on helping you identify the key people who are going to serve as your support connections throughout this program. We call them OGs.

Opportunity Guides

Let's build your **HUB of OGs**.

I want you to select six gainfully employed people.

These could be people in your family, a former teacher, a counselor, a business owner, a former employer, anyone who has a good job, and who you think would be willing to share some success information with you.

Take your time.

We call these people OGs – Opportunity Guides – people who commit to sharing good info with you about success, education, and work. If they are the same people from the previous exercise, that's fine. Just make sure you list at least six. Then list two positive things about each of them.

Person 1: _____

Two positives about them:

_____

_____

Person 2: _____

Two positives about them:

_____

_____

Person 3: _____

Two positives about them:

_____

_____

Person 4: _____

Two positives about them:

_____

_____

Person 5: _____

Two positives about them:

_____

_____

Person 6: _____

Two positives about them:

_____

_____

Now we are going to take it to another level.

I want you to call each person using the following script. You can personalize it as you deem necessary.

We call this the **YOUTRY Statement.**

> **Hello, _____. It's _____**
>
> **I just enrolled in the workforce success program and I'm trying to (*workforce goal*).**
>
> **I am trying because (*heartfelt message about why you want to reach that goal*).**
>
> **What advice do you have for me on how I can reach it?**
>
> **Thank you.**
>
> **Would you mind if I keep you updated on my progress?**

That's it!! You just learned how to kick off the social capital building process.

Keep going!

Add names to the list until you get six people who responded with a positive yes – "yes you can keep me updated on your progress."

You just opened the door to building a meaningful reciprocal connection with that individual. It's a connection that will open up worlds of opportunities for you as well as others.

Become truly comfortable with your YOUTRY statement. **_Get hype wit it!_** You can even put it out on social media with #makinitnation.

But always remember to practice, practice, practice. Practice using your YOUTRY statement in front of others, the mirror, every chance you get. If you can't go out, then call people. Trust me, it works.

Just listen to their recommendations and keep them updated monthly on what you are doing to achieve your goal. Use the activities in this course to make connections with them. You'll have mad social capital in no time.

The Social Capital Building Process

Now that you identified your HUB of OGs – the six social capital assets who are going to help you on this journey, it's time to start social capital building.

Here's how it works.

Each month that you're in the Workforce and Summer Job Success program and 6 months after, you are going to reach out to an OG and update them on your Workforce Success efforts. Go to _makinitnation.com_ and download the OG Update tool to help you keep track of which OG you've spoken to and when.

It could be an email, a text, a phone call, a shout out on social media...whatever. We will make it easy for you. Many of the activities in this program require you to connect with an OG.

If you start today and keep connecting with an OG for 6 months, where do you think you'll be by the end of the six months?

Yes, you will be possessing a whole lot of social capital that will be instrumental in your job search efforts. But you got this. Workforce Success is yours!

Stepping Stones

Asking OGs how to get a job is a powerful way to get a job.

Let me say that again: ***Asking OGs how to get a job is a powerful way to get a job!***

The truth is, you already know the person who is going to help you get a job, you are just not acting like it.

They say that every person knows about 600 people. That means that you personally have about 600 different connections that can lead to job opportunities.

But if we consider the fact that every one of those 600 people in your circle each has 600 people in their own circles, then ***you actually have 360,000 possible connections.***

Everybody in your life, whether they are connected to you directly or not, has the potential to bring a job opportunity your way. All you have to do is go out and establish those connections.

I've seen too many young people ignore these connections. They go put in 20 online applications, but they never speak to their Uncle Joe whose company has 10 job openings.

You must make that social capital jump.

Don't believe me? Let's take rapper 21 Savage for example.

21 struggled with several issues as a kid; behavioral problems, living in a separated family, dealing with gun violence and gangs, in and out of juvie, the madness never seemed to end. Things went from bad to worse on his 21st birthday when he was shot six times and his best friend was killed. Right after, he decided to start rapping in order to deal with the tragedy. But instead of spending countless hours handing out his mixtape to whoever would listen, he turned to his best friend's uncle who was in a position to provide him with the necessary equipment he needed to record music professionally and open up the door to bigger opportunities that would lead to his successful rap career.

Everybody wants to make it on their own, but as you can see, most people don't. They get help from others.

There is another MAKiN' iT Success Law that says: *"Young people who learn through trial and error will always lose to those who learn through others' trial and error."*

Think about it. Why make mistakes that have been made hundreds of times before when you can learn from the people who made those mistakes.

If you make the same mistakes, that's not progress. That is staying stuck - repeating the cycle.

Are you trying to evolve or are you trying to stay stuck?

Are you stuck, and how long have you been stuck in the same situation?

Keep it real. There are people all around you who **aren't** stuck. Yet, you have been following other stuck people.

That's why you are here to build that mental muscle.

That's why we call on others to help you find employment opportunities because that is how most people do it successfully.

Simple!

If you ask people how they got their current job, the majority will tell you that it was through connections, a plug, a hookup, a strong tie, even a weak tie. A strong tie is someone you know on a first name basis and a weak tie is someone your strong tie knows on a first name basis.

hy are you putting more energy into online applications when you have social
pital all around you?

ild it! Evolve!

ive and Free!

out out the response!

ee and Alive!

OG's Shared Knowledge

I'm sure you know by now that workforce success is all about creating and cultivating relationships. Staying connected and implementing the social capital framework is key. This is why at the end of every chapter you will find an "OG's Shared Knowledge" page. This is where you will record the knowledge and advice your hub of OGs gave you as you completed the chapter's activities. As you move through life and journey through the workforce, refer back to these records to give yourself occasional reminders of information and advice you should be applying to your life and remind yourself to keep in contact with the connections you've developed. Be sure to fill out this page before moving on to the next chapter.

This chapter, I added the following people to my hub of OG (write out their names and, if they're not family, how you met them):

_____

_____

_____

We discussed the following topics:

_____

_____

What I learned from these discussions was:

_____

_____

I will contact them every *(how often will you reach out?)* _____

by *(how will you stay in contact; email, phone call, visit, etc.)* _____

Date completed: _____

CHAPTER 2

The New Job Hunt Success Formula

Each year, **hundreds of thousands** of young people nationwide join the workforce. Wanna know how they do it? Believe it or not, there are four major strategies that young folks use to find a job; through their family and friends, through the support of a workforce agency, through the direct approach (like walking up into a company and speaking to the owner, or by filling out an online application).

If you want a job, you should try all of these things, however, there is a way to do it so that you increase your chances of success.

Let me break it down.

- **46%** of your time should be spent on finding job opportunities through family/friends (social capital)

- **28%** of your time should be spent on online applications and job boards (like Snag-a-job, Indeed, Monster, and the others).

- **17%** of your time should be spent receiving the assistance of a job training or an employment agency

- **8 %** of your time should be spent on the direct approach – properly walking into a business and asking the manager if they are hiring.

If you follow this formula, you will ***increase your chances of getting a job 10 times over!***

Now, let's look at ways to put THE NEW JOB SUCCESS FORMULA into action.

Don't Look for Jobs; Have Jobs Look for You

Let's be real - a formula only works if you use it.

There are hundreds of exercise programs, diets, and fitness apps on the market but most people who buy them are still out of shape.

For example, let's say that you've decided to take a 14-day challenge that'll help you lose 20 pounds in two weeks. You've even found an app that tells you exactly how to do it. Sounds great, right!?

But downloading the app and scrolling through its contents isn't going to make you lose the weight. You actually have to do the exercises!

This may seem like a "duh" moment, but this is exactly what some people do when it comes to job hunting.

You have the formula for job success, but simply having it isn't enough. You must put in hard work to get the results and the type of future you want. You can have all the strategies in the world but if you are not actively looking for work, work won't find you.

While you're putting in the work, you will also need to have the right mindset in order to successfully use these job success strategies. You must have a full and clear understanding of your goals and be confident in yourself and what you want to achieve. Only then will your connects, OGs, and future employers see your true potential to not only work hard but succeed at work.

Think of it this way, if you're dieting, shouldn't you begin with a goal weight in mind? You'll need to set a realistic target for you to reach. Once you have that in mind and you know exactly what you want the outcome to be, you'll be more inclined to stay focused and do what it takes to reach that particular goal.

This is what you need to do as you implement the job success strategies. Envision where you'll be five years from now. In a secure job? In college? Owning a home?

Keep this image as a mental poster each time you reach out to an OG, walk into an employment agency, speak directly to a manager, or even fill out an online application. That image is your ultimate goal that will be achieved through job success.

If you follow the advice in this book, you won't have to look for jobs, ***jobs look for you.*** You will become the young person all jobs seek. We will make sure that you'll never have a problem looking for a job again.

Let's dive deeper into the perfect job search formula.

I'm going to walk you through an exercise that will help you develop that necessary Workforce Success focus.

I want you to visualize your ideal life a year from now...

Imagine that you're connected to a group of professionals in a business or organization. You're saying hello to the CEO as she smiles back at you. All the employees appreciate your youthful energy and outlook. You check your bank balance and see that your paycheck was just deposited.

The more details you add, the better. Picture what you're holding in your hand, the kinds of clothes you're wearing, the things that people will say about you. Use all five senses.

Do you have an image in your head? Good.

You are positioning yourself for success by looking beyond the present moment. The more details you offer, the more realistic it will feel. If it feels real, then **you are training your brain to be where you want it to be, not leaving it in the present, but *preparing it for the future.***

Now come back to the present and let's get busy.

One thing we want to be clear about, ***if you want to be present for the future, you must stay alive and free today.***

In the next lesson, we will look at a decision-making tool that will ensure your future success today.

Standing Out with A Success Mindset

If you want to get the most out of this book, you must keep it real with me.

So, let me ask you, have you ever tried to justify a negative action or behavior as survival?

Here are some examples of ways I have heard others try:

- ❖ "I had to fight because I wasn't going to be disrespected."

- ❖ "I wasn't the one who stole, I was just with him."

When did the promotion of death, incarceration, and unemployment become **"survival?"**

If the result is going to jail, losing their life, injuring another, or staying unemployed or underemployed, how is that survival?

As members of the MAKiN' iT Nation, we call that **Falsely Claiming Survival**. Young adults with a success mindset understand the difference between true survival and false survival.

Think about it.

True survival means constantly promoting your life, freedom, and future economic opportunity. To take away from it makes no sense. A major part of the problem is that the word "survival" is ambiguous - it is open to more than one interpretation or can easily have a double meaning.

"Survival" is defined as the act of living longer than another person.

If you interpret this definition to mean the person next to you, then your willingness to survive is based on who you are around. If you are around people surviving day to day, you will be trying to survive day to day. If you are around people trying to survive for future success, you will try to survive for future success.

As members of the MAKiN' iT Nation, we use the Survival Scale to help people develop a new definition of survival to take the ambiguity out of what survival really means. That's why in MAKiN' iT, we always use the words "Alive and Free!"

In our world, *survival is defined as consistently taking steps to promote your life, freedom, and future economic opportunities*, not take away from it.

In the next session, we want you to keep it real and answer a few questions. Let's review them together:

- ❖ Was there a time when you, or someone you know, falsely claimed survival? Who was it and what were the circumstances surrounding the situation?

- ❖ What did you gain? What did you lose?

- ❖ What are you doing now to represent true survival - What's your proof that you are talking the talk and walking the walk?

Acting Consistently Towards Success

We all must take time to evaluate where we are on the MAKiN' it Journey. If we don't know where we are going, any road will take us there. We want you to be focused on success. In order to do so, you need to develop the **success mindset** and we are here to help you do just that.

A major element that helps define the MAKiN' iT mindset is consistency. *Consistency is defined as the quality of always behaving or performing in a similar way.* If you stay consistent towards success, you will be a success.

So why aren't many people successful? Because they're putting consistency towards the wrong thing.

Commitment to the Streets or Workforce Success: Where are You?

That was work and we know that **_hard work always beats talent especially when talent doesn't want to work hard._**

It is important to evaluate ourselves on a daily basis. Each day there are negative influences that weigh on us, often causing us to make decisions that are not in our best interests. You may wake up feeling like a six but by the end of the day, you're down to a 4. It's important to recognize when the shifts occur so you can take action to restore your settings.

When life beats you down, you must find a strategy to pick yourself up. If the goal is life, freedom, and future economic opportunity, we know the way to go and must find the support and strategies to get us to where we want to be.

Time for another "keep it real" activity!

On the Survival Scale, rate yourself from a one to six, with one representing commitment to the streets and a six representing a commitment to workforce Success.

Remember to keep it real!

My Rating: _____

In the next section, I have a few questions designed to help you get to where you want to go. Let's keep it moving.

Making Connections Work

I want you to think about your rating.

What is the one thing that you can do this week to move up the scale or at least to make sure that you don't lose your position on it? What's a major resource that can help you manage your way up the scale?

I call it **social capital**. Remember, social capital is the value of your connections to individuals, organizations, and institutions. Every member of the MAKiN' iT Nation must be trained on social capital building techniques.

I created the social capital framework about eleven years ago because traditional methods of in-class learning were not effective for many young people.

What many educators fail to realize is that there are people in your community who have overcome many obstacles in life: difficulties in school, discrimination, problems finding a job, homelessness, sexism, drug addiction, and unemployment - who can serve as great sources for learning, support, and opportunity acquisition.

These are the people who will be there for you when school is closed. They are the people who know about available jobs and training opportunities in the area and what to do to prepare for them.

That's why in this Workforce and Summer Job Success guide, we use a social capital framework to push you to make as many positive connections to these individuals in your community as possible. We are also going to push you to jump social distances to make connections with others outside of your community who can expose you to a world that you may have never dreamed of. **Building social capital is the key to success.**

Are you ready to start building it?

Connections

So, let's start building some social capital. Let's turn some contacts into connects.

We're going to focus on making a connection with one gainfully employed peer. This is someone your age who has a job or has recently worked. If you don't know someone personally, ask around for names. Speak to program staff, teachers, and peers. Look to members of your community or family. Examples of working peers are everywhere.

There is a saying that goes, *"If you show us the average income of your five friends, we'll show you your average income."*

Let that sink in for a moment. Your average income is the total average income of five of your friends. See how the people you know, the people you hang around with affects your future and financial opportunity?

Take a moment and think of a young person you hang with who has a job. I want you to reach out to them and ask the following questions. Write their answers below.

What did they do to get the job?

_____

_____

_____

What is/was the most challenging part of the job and how do/did they handle it?

_____

_____

_____

What advice do they have for you about finding a job and being the best worker, you can be?

_____

_____

_____

Go ahead, go out there and get it done.

Welcome to the Starting Line

As a triathlete, I have raced numerous races including three Ironman triathlons where you swim 2.4 miles, bike 114 miles, and run 26.2 miles, all in under 17 hours. I think I know something about hard work and endurance.

In 2012, I faced a life-altering injury that threatened my ability to walk, let alone race again. After undergoing joint replacement surgery and a year of rehab, I started to race again. I was nowhere near as fast as I was, but I still made the distance.

I learned a lot about myself and life during that time. We often think about winning, but that's not what's important. The real test is having the courage to get up and try. We may not win the race, but we can celebrate making it to the starting line. With this guide in hand, you are well on your way to running your own race. So ready yourself at that starting line and be prepared to go full force.

On your mark, get ready, get set, let's go!

OG's Shared Knowledge

In this chapter, I learned about the importance of keeping the right company and spoke to _____ about their current job at _____ as a _____.

They gave me information about:

_____

_____

_____

_____

I also learned:

_____

_____

_____

_____

I plan to apply this knowledge to my life by:

_____

_____

_____

_____

I will update them every _____ on my progress.

Date completed: _____

CHAPTER 3

In this chapter, we are really going to be putting in work. By now, you should have a deeper understanding of the proper mindset and strategies you will need to go out and snatch that future you crave. You've built your social capital and you've found your OGs. Now, let's use all of this knowledge and make things happen.

LESSON ONE: Job Programs

Job programs are part of our country's history, dating back to the Great Depression. Job programs include hundreds of local, private, and nonprofit organizations. Each program offers something slightly different, but they all have one major thing in common - **they prepare you for the world of work.** Job programs are in every major city and accessible in most rural areas. They help businesses meet their needs by recruiting, training, and placing qualified workers within various growth industries.

If you want to be successful in job programs, you must match your interests with the growth industries in your area.

We will help you do that by having you visit *careeronestop.org* and complete a brief career interest assessment. It's a quick and easy assessment and should take you only a few minutes to complete. When you complete the assessment, write down the top five occupations that match your interests. Then I want you to **share this list with your OGs.** Let them know that you just finished a career assessment and that this list is what came up as your main occupational interest areas. Ask them if they know anything about the occupations. Find out if they know anyone who works in these areas. I'll show you how to use that information in the next lesson.

In the meantime, I want you to keep something in mind. To truly secure your financial future, it requires you to take action. It's not enough to just read this book and gain knowledge. You must truly go out and complete the tasks we discuss. Having freedom and financial opportunities won't be handed to you on a silver platter. You have to hustle. You have to connect. You have to talk. You have to discuss. So, whenever I suggest you reach out to your OG or anyone else, do yourself a favor, and actually do it.

LESSON TWO: Occupational Search

What did you discover about your career interests? What info did your OG share with you?

There are thousands of occupations in the U.S. Most people are introduced to an occupation through a friend or a family member. Without that introduction, you may never know about all the career possibilities that await you.

For example, did you know that an elevator mechanic is a growing occupation with great pay that only requires a high school diploma plus some training?

Get out there and connect yourself to different people in diverse occupational areas. By doing so, you will connect yourself to the nebulae of networks where most opportunities are born.

I want you to go back to *careeronestop.org* and click on the occupation and you'll see a detailed profile that breaks down everything from the average pay to the future job outlook. Go through every detail. Pay attention to the sections where they tell you about local training and work opportunities in your area.

I want you to **contact these organizations using your YOUTRY statement** and start the social capital building process. Try to add two more OGs to your list while in the process. You might not be ready to pursue the occupational area, but it never hurts to have someone in your corner when you are.

LESSON THREE: How to Choose the Right Training Program

Let's look at some program basics.

There are two basic types of programs: **subsidized programs** and **unsubsidized programs**.

Subsidized programs are programs where your wages and some of the costs for your employment are paid by a government agency or a non-profit organization. Subsidized programs are designed to ensure that all youth get an opportunity to develop much-needed work experience. Most subsidized placements are in the public sector (federal, state, city, and non-profit institutions). A major perk of subsidized programs is the connections that you can make if you need additional services and support. Subsidized programs are geared toward young women, communities of color, people with disabilities, previously incarcerated, and more.

Unsubsidized programs are ones where all costs of your employment are handled by the employer and the workforce agency assumes the responsibilities of providing you with job coaching and support services. Unsubsidized programs are harder to come by and are very competitive.

Both types of programs usually combine opportunities for education, leadership, skill-building, and credentialing.

Whatever avenue you choose to take, know that you have options out there – probably more than you thought. If you are not connected to a workforce or summer job program, or if you are interested in learning about other workforce services in your area, in the next section I will give you a link to a website where you can search workforce programs by city, state and zip code. Each workforce agency has experts on staff that can guide you and your family through the range of summer and year-round work experience and training opportunities available in your city.

Before you contact the program, though, let me walk through some questions that I highly recommend you ask.

- ❖ What programs or services do you offer for X-year-olds (enter your age)?

- ❖ How does the program define success and what is the success rate?

- ❖ What are three things that most young people like about your program?

- ❖ What are three things that they don't like?

- ❖ What opportunities are there to gain industry-recognized credentials?

- ❖ How many work experience sites do you have and how do you determine who is selected for those sites?

- ❖ What is the payment schedule and how much are we paid?

- ❖ Are there any scholarship opportunities for future education?

What other questions do you want to ask? Write them down below and get started making your calls.

_____

_____

_____

_____

_____

_____

LESSON FOUR: Occupational Searching

I hope you made some good contacts. Remember, every time you go out, you are building social capital. Get the contact information of every person you meet and keep them updated on your progress.

Your goal is to build past your six OGs. **We want you to develop and maintain connections with 24 people every six months.** As an Opportunity Seeker, your goal is to find positive opportunities to earn and learn. This is the quickest and simplest way to reach your goal. I have done this activity with over 1000 people and it's amazing how many people struggle to list just 24 names. We always say, "you don't know who you know."

Let's come up with a list of 24 people who you know. To make this exercise easier, we are going to break the 24 into two groups: the first group of 12 are people in your community, friends, family, former teachers, etc. Contact the person and inform them that you are part of the Workforce and Summer Job Success program and that you would like to ask them a few questions:

❖ Where can a person my age work or find job training in this city? What type of connections do you have there and if so, may I have their contact information?

❖ Where are the good jobs in this city?

❖ What makes them good?

❖ What skills and credentials do I need to get these jobs?

❖ What recommendation(s) do you have for me on how to achieve workforce success?

❖ Would you mind if I keep you updated on my progress?

Now, let's make it happen. In the next lesson, you're going to build your list. Try to list twelve people that you've been in contact with at least twice within the past full year. Go ahead, get 'er done.

LESSON FIVE: You Don't Know Who You Know

For the second list, I want you to focus on 12 businesses in your city. It could be any business. You can choose the ones that you frequent or the ones where you would like to work.

For example, if you always wanted to work at the Apple store, then visit the Apple store. If you are interested in securing a job at Footlocker, then visit Footlocker. Someone is waiting to help a young Opportunity Seeker like yourself. Don't deny them the opportunity to do so.

Like the first list, I want you to contact these businesses, inform them that you are part of the Workforce and Summer Job Success program, and ask them the following questions. Feel free to add your own.

❖ What job opportunities are available at this company for a hardworking and dedicated X-year-old?

❖ What are the entry requirements?

❖ What is the first step that I should take if I am interested in a summer job opportunity here?

❖ How could a responsible young person like me benefit this company?

❖ (If available) May I apply for a position?

❖ May I keep you connected on my workforce development progress?

Do you think this is hard? I think wasting your time is hard if you are not willing to go out there and build social capital. If you want a job, looking for a job is a full-time job and you need to start building social capital. So, embrace the search and everything that comes with it.

Think big. By the end of this exercise, you should have 24 connects to help you reach workforce success. Make sure you have each persons' contact information to keep them updated on your progress.

Add me to the list if you want some motivation to get it done. In fact, you will be able to add the whole MAKiN' iT Team and join us on our special website for additional training, conferences, and special events.

Next up we'll go through how to look for the job search.

LESSON SIX: Looking the Part

If you are serious about building social capital, you must check your **"12, 12, 6"**. Here in the MAKiN' iT Nation, the first twelve is how you look from 12-feet away (your dress, walk, confidence), the second twelve is how you are sensed from 12 inches away (your smell, look of your eyes, your facial expression) and the six represents the first six words out of your mouth.

For example, I am wearing black dress pants; a white, button-down shirt; black socks; and black dress shoes. My eyes will be clear, I will smell good (don't use cologne or perfume, just use soap). I look friendly and I'm smiling while holding my head up and walking toward my connect. I will stop short about six feet away and say, "Hello, my name is Ed DeJesus. I'm sorry we can't shake hands but I wanted to let you know that it is a pleasure to meet you."

Are you ready?

Next, I want you to work on building your 12, 12, 6. If you are missing anything, take the time to acquire that item. If you're struggling with a behavior, such as looking the connect in the eye, then practice, practice, practice. If you need to work on that smile—practice. You may see yourself extending a business card, but you don't have one. Then go make one. If you see yourself wearing Khaki pants and shoes, but you don't have any, then go to a thrift store and get some. Ask for dress shoes for your birthday. I guarantee it - if you ask any OG to help you get dress shoes for an interview, they will find a way to help.

Just don't ask for dress shoes while you are wearing $200 sneakers.

Seriously, are you trying to make it or fake it?

If you work these things out beforehand, your 12, 12, 6 will be smooth. More importantly, making connections will be easy, plus you will be more confident.

That's right! Get your OG involved. They already know that you are an Opportunity Seeker trying to make successful moves. Don't you think that they'll be honored to help you look the part?

If you don't know what appropriate dress is, just holler at my girl Yo-UTU-be. We call her YOUTUBE on the block. She's got you!

OG'S Shared Knowledge

In this chapter, I developed my list of occupations and reached out to the following organizations:

_____

_____

_____

Out of this group of organizations, I felt most comfortable and connected with *(write the name of the company):*

_____

_____

At this place, I spoke to _____ and they told me:

_____

_____

_____

I plan to keep this connection and foster the relationship by:

_____

_____

And reach out every: _____

I also learned about the importance of keeping up with my image. I

asked one of my OGs, _____ for help. They helped me by:

_____

_____

Date completed: _____

CHAPTER 4

As I've said before, this guide was not made to help you **get a job**; it was written to help you **<u>do your job</u>**. Don't worry, I'll help you get that money too. That's the easy part.

The hard part is getting that money and managing the multiple jobs that you already have. It's hard to earn money and still be a great student. It's hard to chase cash and earn credentials. It's hard to grind and still build social capital. The challenge is to make sure that making money doesn't interfere with your FEO, AKA future economic opportunity.

There are many reasons why you may want a job, and all of them are valid. Most often, young people who are looking for a job have one thing in mind: *getting that paper*. But have you stopped to consider the other benefits of a job?

To get started, let's work on your role statement. I'll do mine and you can complete yours in the next section. For example:

I am a **father**.

I am a **youth advocate**.

I am a **husband**.

Now, I'm going to add a description of how work can help me in these roles. For example.

I am a **father** and I want to work because **I want to provide the best for my wife and kids**.

I am a **youth advocate** and I want to work **because I want to help millions of young people stay alive, free, and develop future economic opportunity.**

I am a **husband** and I want to work because **one day I want to retire with my wife and relax.**

Your turn.

Don't think about it too hard –write down what comes to mind. Afterward, I want you to speak to an OG about why they work and create a "WHY THEY WORK POSTER." You can use whatever material is lying around the house. Get creative. Take a picture of your poster and post on social media with the hashtag *#makinitnation*.

I am sure this will be fun plus you can send it to your OG as a gift. It is a great way to keep the social capital building process going.

I am a _____.

I am a _____.

I am a _____.

How can work help you achieve these goals?

I am a _____ and I want to work

because_____.

I am a _____ and I want to work

because_____.

I am a _____ and I want to work

because_____.

In the next lesson, we will review the 5 things every Opportunity Seeker should get from work experience.

It's called FEO, it's time to act like you know.

Meaning

There are many reasons why people work and *"Meaning"* is #1.

Research shows that people are even willing to give up some of their compensation for greater meaning at work. People want meaning so badly that they were willing to pay for it.

I know you are asking, "What is 'meaning'?"

Meaningful work is work that helps you better understand or achieve your purpose in life. Put it like this: you have a better chance of finding success with meaningful work than with work that you find meaningless.

This is why we focus so much on your roles. If you place work in the context of your roles there is a greater likelihood that you will find that work meaningful.

Let's do an activity together. I'll go first, then you follow my lead.

Let's imagine having a job that we find meaningful. Let's describe this job and the work it would entail.

Briefly describe a job that you find meaningful.

What job do you find meaningful?

_____

_____

_____

What does that job entail? In other words, what are some of the things you will have to do in this job?

_____

_____

_____

_____

Skills

At MAKiN' iT Nation, we promote future economic opportunities (FEO), not jobs. As stated earlier, a job will not lead you to success but FEO will. There are five main components of FEO.

The first component: ***skills***.

Skills are what helps you pay the bills. A skill is something you do exceedingly well.

I know you have skills but do you have the skills that can land you a job? That's what we call a workplace skill. Workplace skills are the abilities you need to successfully accomplish work tasks. And the truth is, many young people lack real workplace skills. Do you have workplace skills? Let's see what you got!

I can't see you, so, I'm going to have to trust that you are doing the exercise. Just remember that this is all to help you and to get all you can out of this book, you'll need to truly complete the exercises.

So, I'm going to ask you a question. The goal is to answer the question in a full sixty seconds without saying "um", "ah", and "annnn". Get out your phone and set the timer for 60 seconds. You ready?

Start!

Why should I hire you?

How do you think you did?

Did you hear many ums, ahs, and annns?

Well, I heard them.

Nah, I'm just messing with you. But get this, 85% of the young people we challenged with this test can't pass.

Why? It's simple; they just don't practice.

A skill is simply a repetitive action that you do over and over. If you care about skill-building, you should practice, practice, practice. If you practice answering interview questions, then you will be good at interview questions. Easy as that.

Your speaking will automatically improve, and you'll be more comfortable in an interview setting.

But let me ask you a question, and I want an honest answer.

How many hours a week do you practice interviewing?

Later we will tell you about our 2/1/66 skill development formula that'll help you own the entire interviewing process.

Uncovering Your Skills

Are you ready to continue? Good!

Another important workforce skill is *time management*. Having poor time management skills is the quickest way to get fired. When you know how to balance your time, take care of your tasks, and hold yourself accountable, every other aspect of workforce success becomes easier.

There are too many workplace skills to cover in this book, however, I can give you a good strategy for skill development.

We call it **"Ask An OG."** This the second-best way to find out about the skills you'll need to succeed.

The number one best way to find out about the required skills is by speaking directly to an employer. If you know the skills required for the job, then you can work directly on developing those skills. If an OG or employer told you the skills required for the job, and you went out and mastered those skills, where do you think you'll be on the employment line? You'll probably be the first one to get the job. There are other ways to identify workplace skills. Here are a few:

- ❖ Look at the job description

- ❖ Research the position online

- ❖ Speak to current employees

Understanding the Job Description

A good way to find out about the required skills is the job description. The **job description is an internal document that tells you about the essential skills, job duties, and job responsibilities for the position.** Employers don't have to provide job descriptions, but it is good workplace practice if they do so. If they don't, you should ask the employer for a written job description so you can be clear about your duties and the requirements of the position. Just be aware that not everything is on the job description. **You must be flexible.**

Download the sample Job Description on the MAKiN' iT Nation website and circle any references to the skills needed to perform the job.

In the event that there is no job description and the employer won't provide one for you, then you can research the position online. I recommend ONET but there are tons of other websites that you can check out.

ONET provides a lot of details on the requirements of a wide variety of positions. If ONET is a little too complicated, try *careeronestop.com*. This website has videos and can even connect you to companies hiring in your city. This is a great resource to use to learn about workplace skills and companies that require those skills. Now, I want you to identify ten websites that can teach you about career information, I just gave you two, now add eight more.

1. _____ https://www.onetonline.org/find/ _____

2. _____ https://www.careeronestop.org/ _____

3. _____

4. _____

5. _____

6. _____

7. _____

8. _____

9. _____

10. _____

The final strategy is to speak to current employees about the skills required for the position.

It is easier than you think. All you need to do is to pick up the phone and ask. Call the company directly and ask for someone in the department. Tell them that you are a student in the Workforce Success program and that you would like a minute of their time to get some information on the skills necessary for a specific position. Remember that some will help you out, some won't; but so what? It doesn't matter – someone is always waiting to help out a young adult and that young adult is you.

Building Socio-Emotional Skills

There are other types of skills that are just as important. They are called **social-emotional skills**. Social-emotional skills are the skills needed for managing emotions, maintaining positive relationships, and making responsible decisions. Basically, they are the skills you need so you don't go throwing away your life, freedom, and future economic opportunity.

Alive and Free, baby! That's how we roll!

Let's look at the five social-emotional skills areas:

1. Self-Awareness

This skill is about how well you can look at your emotions and values and see how they impact your behavior. By analyzing yourself honestly, you can begin to let go of the **"stinking thinking"**. Having good self-awareness puts you in a growth mindset instead of in a fixed mindset.

Good examples of self-awareness skills are being able to identify one's triggers, understand personal strengths, and being able to label one's emotions.

Let me give you an example:

A 9-grader, who is anxious about starting her summer job, thinks about her 8th-grade graduation when she had to speak in front of the entire school. She remembered how she got rid of the fear by repeating a poem that her mother often shared with her. By doing so, she gave a great speech which got her a lot of praise and encouragement. So, instead of fearing her new summer job, she just thought of how she overcame fear at her 8th-grade graduation and all she gained by doing so. Now she is excited about her first day of work and is ready to gain even more.

2. Social Awareness

Social awareness is how well you recognize social codes for behavior. You must be able to recognize the social codes that promote ***death, unemployment, and incarceration***. That is what we call D.U.I. I am big on awareness of social codes because it impacts how you act in certain situations. Remember, if it doesn't promote life, freedom, and future economic opportunity, it isn't survival. Having social awareness of what is true survival and what isn't, is the key to lifelong success. If you get it twisted, you may pay a big price.

We hope you join the MAKiN' iT nation so we can teach you more about our Survival Laws and help you make major survival moves.

3. Self-Management

Self-management helps you keep emotions in check, manage stress, and communicate your needs calmly and clearly. This is the difference between causing fistfights or walking away with a clear head. In the world of work, it can mean the difference between losing your job and getting that promotion. Studies have shown that people with self-management skills are more successful in work and life. In MAKiN' iT, we talk about the difference between an ***immediate results mindset*** and a ***delayed results mindset.*** Which one do you have?

It all goes back to the survival mindset.

When you're in survival mode and caught in an immediate-results environment, the wants of today become stronger than the glimmering promise of tomorrow. You develop immediate-results habits, reinforced by a society that glorifies the fast, the now, and the moment.

The problem is that the first prerequisite for workforce success is shifting that mindset to a delayed-results one. Developing a delayed-results mindset is challenging; many people get caught up in an environment that doesn't encourage new habits. It's tough when we're constantly hit by forces pushing an immediate pleasure-seeking mentality, whether it comes from your friends who want to get high today, a parent who just wants you to bring home some cash, or a school that just cares about test scores.

These forces weigh against your success because they promote the wrong mindset. You need a delayed-results mindset.

Let's take a look at Opportunity Seeker Ali's Situation:

> *Each morning, Ali promised himself that he would go out and find a job. All he did was scroll through his social media pages for a quick dopamine hit (that natural chemical that floods your body and makes you think you're happy). When he did roll into class, he would spend 60% of his day looking at his phone or daydreaming about that wicked game of Fortnite waiting for him. He'd head home, abandon the idea of homework, and spend the night switching between video games and social media. In bed, he'd promise himself that he'd go out and find a job the next day only to wake up and repeat the same routine, day in and day out.*

Did Ali have a delayed result or immediate result mindset?

Immediate, of course!

Ali was only focused on giving himself what he wanted at that moment. Even though he temporarily thought about the future by claiming he would go find a job, his actions did nothing to lead to positive results in the future.

4. Decision Making

No matter what some people say, making the right decision isn't always easy. Parents and teachers love to tell young folk that "all you had to do was *decide* not to" do something as if it were really just that easy. But we all know that there are so many factors involved in decision making. Perfecting decision making is an absolutely necessary skill to have in work and life as a whole.

Luckily, there is one main key to becoming a better decision-maker. In order to make the right decisions, you must be able to ***identify the real dangers in your life and learn how to keep those dangers at bay***. It is these dangers that ultimately cause you to be in a situation in which you are tempted to make bad decisions.

These dangers can be just about anything.

It could be your own toxic thoughts, negative energy from people around you. Even the stereotypes society puts on you can be considered a danger if it's fueling your bad decision making.

You have to keep your eyes open to catch these dangers. When you do finally identify them, steer clear of them. Keep from letting them affect you. Once you do this, you will realize that you are in control. When you're in control, you can easily put yourself in better situations where making a bad decision isn't even possible.

This won't be easy, though, and even when you identify dangers, you'll still be faced with circumstances in which the option of making a poor decision is there.

If this happens, you have to turn it into mind over matter. Fight the urge to make a bad decision by thinking clearly. Forget what you desire and think about what'll happen if you decide poorly.

If you're ever stuck and you're not sure how to make the right decision, hit up one of your OGs. That's what they are there for.

5. Relationship Skills

Building healthy and rewarding relationships with a diverse group of people is critical to success. Through making a variety of friends, you learn how to communicate better, listen well, and cooperate with folks who are different from you. This entire guide is strategically having you build relationships with your OGs – a major step towards healthy and rewarding relationships.

This is what social capital is all about. It's the meaningful relationships that will help you make it to the top.

It's not just enough to grab someone's contact info and put it in your phone. You actually have to follow up with that contact. You gotta make sure you are on their mind. Your name needs to pop up in their heads when they see a particular job opening or opportunity.

Now how is that supposed to happen when they've only spoken to you once or twice? They ain't thinking about you! But that job opening they came across will be snatched by someone else they know.

The bottom line is this: Anytime you don't follow up with a contact or stay connected, that's several opportunities gone. Anytime you refuse to talk to a potential connect, that's several jobs that could have been yours going to someone else.

I know it sounds a bit dramatic, but that's just what it is. This is the truth. While these relationships can bring you success, it's up to you to foster those relationships, make them grow, and make them meaningful.

S.M.A.R.T Skills

The skills we just discussed are absolutely necessary for your recipe for success, yet, there is one secret ingredient that we just can't do without.

I'm talking about **_S.M.A.R.T_** skills.

S.M.A.R.T skills are a set of **S**pecific, **M**easurable, **A**chievable, **R**ealistic, and **T**ime-bound skills that you'll need in order to properly do your job.

Let's break it down:

❖ **Specific:** *These are skills that are specific to a certain job or task.*

For example, if you are assigned the task of monitoring shipments and their monetary value (how much money the shipments are worth) at a department store, you'll need to have good mathematical skills. This skill is very specific to the task at hand.

❖ **Measurable:** *These are skills that can be measured to help track your progress.*

It's one thing to identify and begin developing necessary skills and another thing to know how far you've gotten in your journey toward mastering it. You want to work on skills that allow you to clearly see your progress.

Let's go back to the example about monitoring shipments. Building your math skills are easily measurable. If you're practicing simple addition, subtraction, multiplication, and division problems, over time you will begin to notice that you're getting faster and faster at calculating those shipments at work.

❖ **Achievable:** *Achievable skills are skills that are truly within your reach.*

These skills can be simple ones like being detail-oriented or managing large teams. Even if you do not currently possess these skills, they can be easily obtained through hard work and practice. But the bottom line is that they are within reach.

❖ **Realistic:** *These are skills that are true to what you are capable of.*

We love to big ourselves up, especially when applying for jobs, but we have to be real with ourselves and identify skills that we

ACTUALLY have or can get. To be realistic, a skill must be practical, something that you are willing and able to develop. This isn't just about your personal abilities either. Realistic skills are often based on what you can get your hands on and what you have access to. You'll have a hard time developing computer programing skills if you can't get access to a computer.

❖ **Time-bound:** *Time-bound skills are skills that you can develop in a timely manner.*

We always have room to grow. Developing new skills or strengthening old ones is something we should never stop doing. Yet, being able to do this within a reasonable amount of time is important. You don't want to spend too much time working on a skill. You never know how long a particular opportunity will stick around, so it's best to work on realistic skills within a reasonable time frame.

Here is a template for you to create your SMART skill.

I will [insert skill goal here] by [insert how you will develop the skill]. I will know I am making progress because [insert how you will measure the skill] for [insert time goes here].

Here is my example:

I will *learn how to type* by *practicing on "typing tutor" 15 minutes each weekday and practicing for one hour on the weekends. I will do this by cutting back on video games and social media.* I will know that I am making progress because *I will be able to type fifty words per minute with zero errors* by *May 10*.

Do your best to create your SMART skills statement based on the example above. Meet with an OG for help.

I want you to **choose two skills to work on every thirty days** and write those skills on your master skills list below. Once you have completed the list, share it with your instructor and classmates.

Skill	Date Started	Date Mastered

Do the same for habits.

A habit is a usual way of behaving. Habits are routines done on a regular basis - patterns that we adopt in life. Some habits promote life, freedom, and future economic opportunity and others don't.

People used to say that it takes 30 days to build a habit, but research now states it takes 66 days for a new behavior to become automatic.

So, start identifying those good "alive and free" habits and start building on them each day for 15 minutes a day for the next 66 days. That's what we call the *2/1/66 formula*. **Work on two new skills and one new habit every 66 days.**

Keep track of how much you do each day and stay focused. If you miss a day, start back at zero. Ask an OG to be your accountability partner so they can help you stay on track. Treat yourself if you accomplish the goal and give something up if you don't.

Habit	Date Started	Date Mastered

This is your life and only you can change. Change does not come easy. The more and more you do something, the easier it gets. That's why we want you to go hard. In a few weeks, you will have new skills or habits that you won't remember developing.

Once you complete this, be sure to congratulate yourself. There's no better feeling than be truly proud of yourself because of your hard work.

Learning About Credentials

Now let's go over the second key element of FEO – **_Credentials_**.

A credential is a certification issued by a third party indicating that you are proficient in a certain skill or task. Put simply, a credential is proof provided by someone that tells others you're good at a particular thing.

Examples of credentials include HVAC certification, Commercial Driver License, Forklift Operator, and hundreds of others.

You can earn most credentials in less than one year; some require up to two years. There are many credentials that you can earn in under six months as well.

When you have ideas of the kinds of credentials you need for success, and a plan to get them, your path to success becomes much clearer. You can lock in and do what you got to do to succeed. Credentials will help you move through life with confidence not to mention that it'll make you more qualified for certain jobs. Having a credential gets you one step closer to getting a job.

By having a job, you have the opportunity to learn about credentials every day.

Just ask the people you work with where they got their credentials. Did they go to school, take an online course, or study from a book? This strategy is amazing because if it worked for them, it would work for you too. Plus, you'll know where to get the credential.

Don't waste your time chasing a credential if you don't have a connect who will help you put that credential to work. There are too many young people walking around with credentials that they can't put to use because they don't have the right connection or they have the wrong credential.

In the next section, I want you to speak to one of your OGs about credentials. Which ones do they recommend? Then research those credentials and share your research with your OG.

You want to be down, right! As a future MAKiN' iT Nation member, you got to put in work. ***Hard work beats talent especially when talent does not want to work hard.***

Building Work Experience

There's not much worse than having a blank resume and no references. Having a job gives you work experience to list on your resume. If you struggle to score that first paid opportunity, consider volunteering – it's a powerful way to make connections and fill that resume without constantly facing rejection.

The third FEO element - Work experience - is more than a resume filler, though. It's a way to identify the career that you want to develop. It helps you identify the work that you want to do. Can you be on a computer all day? Make cold calls to strangers? Lead a team of workers? Working a job can help you determine the type of work that you want to do in your future.

Take Linda, for example. She hadn't been doing well in school, but always figured she'd work with kids in a daycare – crafting, playing dress-up, and monitoring naptime sounded easy enough, right? Linda waited until barely graduating high school before applying for jobs working with kids. Once she got hired and started the job that was supposed to be her dream, she realized she hated working with kids – they sneezed all the time, were rude, and got paint on her clothes. But because Linda hadn't explored her options earlier, she felt trapped in the childcare industry, unsure of what else she'd like to do.

What if Linda had gone ahead and worked at a day camp the summer between her junior and senior years? If she'd done that, she may have realized then that kids weren't her cup of tea. Instead, although Linda was frustrated to realize that her daydream hadn't been as fun as she'd hoped, she would have had her last year of high school to consider her options. While she'd been working at the summer camp, maybe the only thing she'd really enjoyed was the fabric arts classes. With that knowledge, she could have looked at programs and enrolled in courses in this area. Eventually, she could have worked her way through community college classes and certifications to study costume design in college – and eventually work in Hollywood. All because she'd decided to try out a summer job and identify her strengths, she gave herself options that created financial economic opportunities that eventually led to her success.

If you want a real-life example, let's take a look at Ryan Coogler. Most people know him as the young black director of Black Panther, Creed I and II, and Fruitvale Station. Before Coogler directed his first feature film, Fruitvale Station, he was an amateur indie filmmaker making his way through college. Though he was playing football at the time, he truly wanted to be a filmmaker and director. But we all know that no-name artists don't stand a chance at profiting from their work, yet he didn't let that stop him. Instead of being worried about making projects that would make a profit, he simply hustled and made his independent films to build his catalog and gain work experience. The time that he spent gaining experience is what caught A-list actor and director Forrest Whitaker's attention that led to Coogler getting the funding and backing he needed to create Fruitvale Station.

Clearly, there are other options for getting work experience than a paid job. Speak to an OG about unpaid work experience opportunities in your city. Believe me, they will be impressed.

Let's move on to the fourth FEO element – Education.

Get the Right Education

If you put the energy into landing a job that works for you, you'll narrow down the educational opportunities that support your advancement in that field. Like with credentials, your co-workers can let you in on the type of education that you'll need to succeed. Sometimes it's not much at all. Be brave enough to ask questions, like, what schools your coworkers went to and why they recommend them (or don't). The power is in your hands. Talk to the people in your life and come up with at least five educational opportunities. They could be as small as taking a 3-month online course or as big as enrolling in a community college. Be sure to let them know what you want to do with your life to get specific suggestions. Write them below and use this list to turn these opportunities into reality.

1. _____

2. _____

3. _____

4. _____

5. _____

Contacts to Connects

You know what the last FEO element iş, right?

Social Capital!

While having a plug in the burger industry may not sound important to your dream career in music production, you might be surprised. Not only may your coworkers know people in the industry, but they can also act as a reference as you move toward your dreams.

Throughout the Workforce and Summer Job Success guide, you build social capital by strategically staying connected to your OGs. However, there is so much more to social capital than we can fit into this book. Check out our Social Capital Builders program for more information. You can find it at *ededucates.com.*

OG's Shared Knowledge

Based on what I learned in this chapter, I've been brainstorming about my skills and how to obtain them. I spoke to OG _____ about my skills list and they said:

_____

_____

_____

I also asked _____ to be my accountability partner.

To obtain the credentials I need for my career, I spoke to

_____ and they suggested:

_____

_____

To develop work experience, I spoke to _____

and they told me:

_____

_____

With this information, I am going to: *(Write out a comprehensive plan describing the steps you are going to take to get work experience and proper credentials. Give yourself a due date for each part of the plan)*

_____

_____

I will keep them updated on my progress every _____

Date completed: _____

CHAPTER 5

You are probably seeing that a lot of prep goes into landing a job and we know that you are excited about the possibilities ahead – a little cash, something for your resume, maybe even a new social life. Remember ... you will not have this job for life – it's just a foundation, a start to building your FEO. We all must start somewhere, and this is your opportunity.

Five Things That You Should Know Before Starting Any Job

Starting a job is fun but you need to go in with a real understanding of what work is like. In this lesson, we will review the five things that you should know before starting any job.

1. Not all jobs are fun

Work is work. It's all about being productive. In return for your productivity, you will get a paycheck. The more productive you are, the more money and opportunities for advancement you should receive. The less productive – well you know what happens then. Focus on being productive- success will follow.

2. You have to Code Switch

"Code-switching" is alternating between two or more cultures. We all do it. For example, company culture includes dressing up in a nice pair of pants and a button-down where school culture is jeans and a t-shirt. In the "Set-it Off Pledge" we talk about having Street-side Smarts and Boardroom potential. That's code-switching. Whether you have to switch up your clothes or your mindset, you'll have to make that appropriate change in order to succeed at your job.

3. Showing up on time is key

Being late and missing work is the number one way young people lose jobs. Some people say that success is just showing up. We believe it is more than that, but the point is well taken. You will not be successful if you don't show up to work and show up on time.

4. Develop tough skin

In the workplace, people don't care too much about your feelings. They want to get the job done. You must be able to handle criticism and not take it too personally. If you don't, you may start to resent the workplace and stop showing up. Understand that you are there to work, not to make friends.

5. Getting along to succeed

At the workplace, you must be a team player. Getting along with your co-workers is the key to success. You can't control who your co-workers are. They will be a diverse group of people all with different personalities and different agendas. The fact of the matter is, you may not like a few of them or they may simply rub you the wrong way. Even still, you have to try your best to avoid confrontation and remain civil at all times.

Now that we reviewed the 5 things that you should know before starting a job, I want you to think about each one and rate your ability to do each on a scale from 1 to 6 with one being "needs work" and 6 being "I got this." Afterward, think about the one thing that you can do to improve your ability in each area and discuss it with your OG at your next meeting.

> ❖ **The ability to stay productive...**
>
>   My Rating _____
>
>   I can improve this ability by:
>
>   _____
>
>   _____

❖ **The ability to code-switch...**

My Rating _____

I can improve this ability by:

_____

_____

❖ **The ability to show up on time...**

My Rating _____

I can improve this ability by:

_____

_____

❖ **The ability to develop tough skin...**

My Rating _____

I can improve this ability by:

_____

_____

❖ **The ability to get along with others...**

My Rating _____

I can improve this ability by:

_____

_____

Getting Ready for the Job

In this lesson, we will start looking at job readiness and what it takes to get ready. If you're currently in your first job or haven't gotten a job yet, it's totally okay. We all had to start somewhere.

What most people don't realize is that they **already have some degree of job readiness**. You may have worked as a babysitter. You may code in school. You could be a master at social media marketing.

The following questions will help you uncover your current level of job readiness. Take a moment to briefly answer them.

What are some responsibilities you've had in the past?

_____

_____

_____

_____

What are some of the skills you possess?

_____

_____

_____

Was there a time(s) when you showed dependability?

_____

_____

_____

When did you complete a project?

_____

_____

_____

Who would say something nice about you? What would they say?

_____

_____

_____

_____

Questions like these can help you uncover the skills, talents, and abilities you possess that can lead to workplace success. Employers want you to come job-ready; they don't want to invest in making you job-ready.

Before you start your job search, it is important to take a **_look at yourself and your attitude_**. According to the U.S Department of Labor, "Your attitude is one of the most important things that employers consider when they interview you. Having a great attitude often is as important as having good skills."

Getting started with your job readiness is not an easy task. When job readiness comes up, people often talk about resumes, cover letters, interview skills, and applications, but it is so much more than that. Everything that you have learned thus far is extremely important. They are the difference between just searching for a job and getting a job and even a career.

Actions Speak Louder Than Words

Think back to the exercise where we looked at your life one year from now. Now let's look to the more immediate future, just six months from now. I want you to ask yourself: What do you need to do now to improve your FEO (future economic opportunities)?

Do you have a vision of how you are going to achieve that goal? If you only have a vague idea, don't worry. This guide will get you ready for success. If you're looking to make the biggest splash in your life and really turn things around in six months, you must honestly answer this question: **What do you do that lets people around you know you're serious about working?**

What you do shows others whether or not you are ready for work. I told you earlier, "It's not only what you know or who you know that gets you the job. It's who knows you and who likes you that really makes the difference."

Many people can know you, but they can know you for the wrong reasons.

Take Carlos for example, Carlos was the class clown. Everything to him was a joke. He didn't know when to turn it off and many of his teachers were upset. During Career Day, several employers asked teachers for their recommendations on students who would be great summer employees. Not one teacher referred Carlos. Everybody knew him but few of the teachers appreciated his ill-timed humor and many of his classmates felt the same.

Let's make sure that this doesn't happen to you

Below, you'll see that there are two job-ready assessments: a self-assessment and a third-party assessment. The self-assessment is for you, the third-party assessment is for someone who knows you. These assessments check how prepared you are for employment and how others perceive your job readiness.

Remember, assessments are only effective if you're honest with yourself. The more transparent your answer, the better an idea you'll have of what you need to do to get a summer job. At this stage in your journey, there are no wrong answers – each answer here leads you to your best life and greatest FEO.

For each of these questions, rank yourself using this scale:

1 - My actions and attitudes show that this is **NEVER** true.

2 - My actions and attitudes show that this is **ALMOST NEVER** true.

3 - My actions and attitudes show that this is **SOMETIMES** true.

4 - My actions and attitudes show that this is **OFTEN** true.

5 - My actions and attitudes show that this **ALWAYS** true

Be as honest as possible...

1. **I'm willing and able to show up to work consistently and on time.**

    My Rating _____

2. **I'm willing and able to follow directions.**

    My Rating _____

3. **I'm willing and able to be trustworthy.**

    My Rating _____

4. **I'm willing and able to show up looking professional and with a good attitude.**

    My Rating _____

5. **I'm willing and able to be alcohol and drug-free.**

    My Rating _____

6. **I am willing and able to handle my paycheck responsibly.**

    My Rating _____

7. **I am willing and able to complete high school. If I've left high school, I'm willing and able to obtain my GED.**

    My Rating _____

8. **I am willing and able to work positively and effectively with others.**

    My Rating _____

After rating yourself on each, I want you to think about a few things: Why did you choose that number? Describe a time when you've demonstrated this ability at work, school, or in your community. What can you do to move one number up the scale? Jot down your answer to these questions below for each rating.

Why did you choose that number?	Describe a time when you've demonstrated this ability at work.	What can you do to move one number up the scale?
1		
2		
3		
4		
5		

Why did you choose that number?	Describe a time when you've demonstrated this ability at work.	What can you do to move one number up the scale?
6		
7		
8		

Now it's time for the third-party assessment. Ask an adult who really knows you to complete the assessment below on your behalf. It could be a parent/guardian, OG, teacher, or coach.

Please use the following rating system to rate my attitudes and actions:

1 - My actions and attitudes show that this is **NEVER** true.

2 - My actions and attitudes show that this is **ALMOST NEVER** true.

3 - My actions and attitudes show that this is **SOMETIMES** true.

4 - My actions and attitudes show that this is **OFTEN** true.

5 - My actions and attitudes show that this **ALWAYS** true

Be as honest as possible...

1. **My willingness and ability to show up to work consistently and on time.**

   Your Rating _____

2. **My willingness and ability to follow directions.**

   Your Rating _____

3. **My willingness and ability to be trustworthy.**

   Your Rating _____

4. **My willingness and ability to show up looking professional and with a good attitude.**

   Your Rating _____

5. **My willingness and ability to be alcohol and drug-free.**

   Your Rating _____

6. **My willingness and ability to handle my paycheck responsibly.**

   Your Rating _____

7. **My willingness and ability to complete high school. If I've left high school, I'm willing and able to obtain my GED.**

   Your Rating _____

8. **My willingness and ability to work positively and effectively with others.**

   Your Rating _____

What did you notice? Were your answers dramatically different from those who rated you? Get their recommendations on how you can improve.

Look over all your answers and write down the average of all the scores you gave yourself. To do that, add up each rating, and divide it by the number of questions (eight).

My Average Job-Readiness Score _____

The answer you get is your actual readiness on a scale of 1 to 5. If you're better off than you thought, then congratulations! If not, we got some work to do.

Now let's figure out how to improve your rating.

Always Room to Improve

Never ever forget that there is _**always**_ room to improve. If you're disappointed to see your average so low, think about the simple changes you can make, and what your life will be like if you make those changes.

You can move up the scale and I'll show you how.

First, choose two areas from the assessment that you will work on. Then speak to another OG about ways you can improve and ask for their help in doing so.

Here's some advice on how to improve in a specific area:

❖ **Willing and able to show up to work consistently and on time**

Attendance and punctuality play a huge role in job success. It is important for you to attend work as scheduled and to arrive at least 15 minutes ahead of time in order to tend to any personal needs before start time. Failure to do so impacts productivity and it creates a problematic work environment.

Most people don't want to be late but are because of bad scheduling. Speak to an OG about what they do to get to work on time and model after them.

❖ **Willing and able to follow directions**

Not following the directions of your supervisors could be costly. Mistakes can be made that cost the company time, money, and reputation. When a supervisor gives you direction, it is usually based on best practices – things that have worked at the company before. Even if you think your idea on the way to do things is better, the company's way has a track record and yours doesn't. Following directions is hard when directions are not well communicated, which happens often. It is your job to make sure that the directions are understood, even if you must ask questions repeatedly in order to clarify your task.

❖ **Willing and able to be trustworthy**

Trust is the ability to allow someone to count on you to do what you agreed to do. If you take a job, your employer is trusting you to get the job done. You're trusting your employer to have your paycheck ready and they are trusting you to do the job so they can give you a paycheck.

❖ **Willing and able to show up looking professional and with a good attitude**

Earlier, we talked about code-switching and its importance. When you work for a company, you represent their brand, not yours. Even after work, your actions could have a major impact on a company's reputation.

❖ **Willing and able to be alcohol and drug-free**

A job is not a way for you to support a drug or alcohol hit. According to the National Survey on Drug Use and Health, about 1 in 13 working adults has an alcohol use disorder. Alcohol and drug abuse by employees result in lost productivity, injuries, and an increase in health insurance claims.

If you have a drug or alcohol problem, address it. There are tons of resources that could help you get on the right track. You always start with your family or OG. They'll more than likely have your back unconditionally and help you without judgment.

❖ **Willing and able to handle my paycheck responsibly**

No one is going to tell you what to do with your money but there are some good recommendations. First and foremost, DO NOT spend your money on the subject we just covered. Secondly, save 10% of what you take home for rainy days. I know it's hard to save but emergencies always pop up and it's good to be prepared for them. Don't take your money and buy things that can hurt your life, freedom, and future economic opportunity. That's not survival, that's stupidity.

❖ **Willing and able to complete high school. If I've left high school, I'm willing and able to obtain my GED**

As we said earlier, a job is not the key to success. Investing in your life, freedom, and FEO is. A job is just a way to get work experience, skills, and build more social capital. Education is the key and working more than 20 hours a week greatly affects your ability to get an education and the likelihood that you will complete it. The payoff of having a high school diploma compared to not having one is $410,000 over your lifetime. A college degree brings in $1 million more than just a high school diploma. Education is important, so make sure you are invested in it and not just work.

❖ **Willing and able to work positively and effectively with others**

Getting along with co-workers is an essential skill for workplace success. Remember, you are going to be around these people 8 hours a day. Having a good relationship with them is key to making the job a place where you want to be. Here are some things to consider: don't share too much personal information especially political and religious beliefs. That could be a landmine. Also, don't get involved in other people's drama. Spilling tea at work is never a good idea because it will only lead to a confrontation that'll go beyond just arguing with co-workers. Gossiping can lead to you being fired or worse, it can spill into your life, and next thing you know, someone else's problems have become your own. Finally, be good at what you do but don't do the work of others. It may seem like you're being productive or helpful when completing other people's tasks, but that's a good way to step on toes and possibly open the door for jealousy among coworkers.

Job Readiness in Action

Now that you completed the Job Readiness Assessment and spoke to a few of your OGs about ways to improve, it's time to put it all into action.

Improving your job-readiness can't be done in one fail swoop. On the contrary, it will take baby steps. In MAKiN' iT Nation, baby steps refer to actions that can be completed in less than two weeks.

With this in mind, I want you to think about the types of baby steps you can take that'll lead to a good job-readiness score.

Answering the questions below will help you put in place an actionable plan. Before you do that, though, I want you to remember a few things:

First, take a moment to contemplate on the questions to allow yourself to give them some real thought.

Secondly, keep in mind what you learned about S.M.A.R.T skills. These attributes should be applied to your baby steps to ensure they can be easily accomplished.

And lastly, keep an open mind. You may think of an out-of-the-box baby step that's crazy enough to work. If so, go for it! You're here to impress yourself and no one else, so make sure you are happy with your plan of attack and proud of your resolve to truly complete them.

What are three baby steps you can take to improve your job readiness?

1. _____

_____

2. _____

_____

3. _____

_____

Identify potential barriers that could stop you from completing the baby steps.

_____

_____

_____

How can you overcome many of these challenges? Feel free to get ideas from peers and family members.

_____

_____

_____

_____

What can you do to make sure you complete your baby steps?

_____

_____

_____

_____

It's up to you to take the baby steps. I am sure some of your OGs would be willing to help, but ultimately, it's on you. You have family and peers who did it. If they share success strategies on how to do it, you'll know that you can do it too.

Make sure you speak with your OG about the work you need to do.

OG's Shared Knowledge

This chapter helped me to zero in on my abilities to be "job ready". I spoke to one of my OGs _____ about my personal assessment and asked them to take it on my behalf. Based on their answers, I learned:

_____

_____

_____

I also spoke to _____ about ways I could improve my job readiness. They suggested:

_____

_____

With this information, I am going to: *(Write about the actions you will take based on the suggestions given to you by your OG)*

_____

_____

_____

_____

_____

_____

I am going to keep them updated on my progress every _____.

Date completed: _____

CHAPTER 6

I don't know about you, but I think it's about time we work to help you master the job-hunting process so you will never be without a job again. Sound good? Great! Let's do it.

To get a job, you could go out there and drop resumes at every company within earshot. Yeah, good luck with that.

Or you could take the time to painstakingly fill out 100 online applications. Good luck with that, too.

How about you stop wasting time and energy on strategies that just don't work?

Instead, dive into your job search with the number one strategy that others use to get jobs - ***social capital***.

Let me show you how.

Did you know that social capital is the number one way to find a job? We covered this in Chapter Two but let's do a quick review.

According to our research, 45% of job seekers get jobs through who they know, while roughly 28% found jobs through job boards and the use of online applications. 17% of job seekers used job agencies, and 8% used the direct approach. That leaves 2% for other methods.

That's the Job Hunt Success Formula.

Basically, I am telling you to **let social capital building be your number one go-to job search strategy.** That's the goal of this course and why it is filled with opportunities for you to connect to Opportunity Guides and others.

In fact, if you had to rate yourself on the survival scale based on your efforts to reach out to OGs, with one being "no effort" and six being "maximum effort", how would you rate yourself?

If you are anything below a 3, I suggest you stop reading right now, flip back to Chapter One, and start all over again. This would prove that you are missing the point of this guide and the duty of every MAKiN' iT Nation member – to build social capital then spend it.

Having people in your corner who see that you're serious about looking for work is your most powerful job search tool. Use it! In fact, the quicker you adopt the Job Hunt Success Formula, the quicker you'll find a job.

Let's review the formula once again:

46% of your job search should be through social capital

28% of your job search should be through job boards

17% of your job search should be through job agencies

8% of your job search should be through a direct approach

We will cover each area in depth. But first, let's look at what prevents some young people from putting the Job Hunt Success formula into action. We call these **Job Hunt Time Wasters** and everybody has some.

Job Search Time Wasters

Now you may be asking, "Ed, now that I have the formula: How much time do I need to invest in it to be successful?" Great question!

We always say looking for a job is a full-time job. If I were to tell you that I spend only two hours a week training for Ironman races, you'd know that I'm not an Ironman triathlete. That type of training will get me no closer to completing a 2.4-mile swim, a 114-mile bike ride, and a 26.2-mile run than doing one push-up a week would get me to Mr. Olympia.

Dr. Ivan Misner, who heads the world's largest connecting organization, BNI, reports that successful connectors spend an average of **six hours a week** participating in connecting activities.

Just to be clear, chatting with your friends on Instagram is not connecting.

In our process, we define connecting as any type of interaction that helps you build social capital with positive, gainfully employed people.

Given that this guide is aimed at young adults, ages 16 to 30, we're going to cut Dr. Misner's recommendation in half. Most of you don't have businesses that you're trying to grow or payrolls that you're trying to meet. Right now, it's all about building your FEO.

In this case, we will recommend thirty-five minutes a day—that's it. Thirty-five minutes a day, five days a week to build a bridge to a great job, a promising career, and untold fortunes. That's not even three hours a week!

Do you have thirty-five minutes a day?

In the next section, you'll look at your biggest time wasters —activities that do not contribute to workforce success. What do you think you'll find?

Thirty-Five Minutes a Day for a Job

How did it go? Did you find the 35 minutes needed to change your future?

I know you can do this because you've already started.

If you are putting work into the Workforce and Summer Job Success Work guide, - you should have more than six people supporting you in your job search efforts. If you are putting in **MAD** work into the Workforce and Summer Job Success process - you should already have a job.

Nobody engages social capital assets like we do.

This is the first workforce development guide built on a social capital framework. It is giving you the opportunity and push to connect with key people who will be instrumental in your success.

So once again, if you haven't made the connections that are built by using this book, I would stop and start over from the beginning.

I want you to make it, not fake it.

If you are ready, let's dive deeper into the number one job search method – social capital building.

A HUB – The Shortest Path to a Job

Did you know that the average person has about 611 connections? And each of those connections has 611 of their own connections. That gives you a network of almost 400,000 people. That's 400,000 connections that you could be making.

The trouble is no one can actually manage 400,000 connections. It would take reaching out to 300 people a day for over three years!

Instead of spamming everyone with emails and calls for years to come, why not focus on developing social capital with a close-knit group of six individuals – who we call your Hub? We touched on this in the earlier chapters, however, now it's time to make your connections count. You must be smart about who you let into your HUB.

According to Robin Dunbar, a British scientist, our brains can only handle meaningful connections with about 150 people – six of which serve as your inner circle. This tells us that *it's not about the quantity of connections you make; it's the quality*. And to maximize your success, your OGs must be top-notch.

Think of your six connects like they're airport hubs. Each connection is a major point that helps you get from one part of the country to another, without having to drive yourself through the distance between each connecting point.

Without these hubs, travel would be a nightmare. Hubs are efficient, saving you time and resources and letting you arrive at your destination as quickly as possible.

Your social hub is no different. They are there to connect you to your goals with the least amount of time and effort. That's why who is in your hub is critical.

Why choose an OG who can only move you one step when you know someone who can move you three?

An ideal hub contains people who not only believe in your potential but have something to offer for your success. They can help you gain information about available jobs, give you the lowdown on career opportunities, and encourage you to push yourself.

These people need to be candid and supportive, willing to share their own experiences, and accept you as you are, and most importantly, aid you in getting to where you want to be.

Much of the work that you have been doing so far has been centered around developing this hub of individuals- OGs. The key to a hub is staying in contact with each person at least once every two weeks.

That's why you often review exercises from this book with a Hub member. The more they see that you are trying, the more likely they are to help.

Next up we are going to take a look at the second most effective job search method – Job Boards.

Using Job Boards Effectively

Job Boards are websites that connect job seekers to available job openings. Businesses use job boards to post openings and job seekers use them to find employment opportunities.

There are regular job boards and specialized job boards.

Specialized job boards focus on a specific industry or occupational areas, like technology, hospitality, and health care. These boards are most used by job seekers who have specific credentials and degrees in a particular sector.

Examples of specialized job boards are ***allretailjobs.com***, ***salesgravy.com,*** and ***healthcarejobsite.com***.

Common job boards, on the other hand, display openings for any and all types of jobs in any field. It's far less specific than specialized boards and has a much larger catalog of job openings.

Examples of common job boards are Indeed, CareerBuilder, Monster, Snag-a-Job.

As an Opportunity Seeker, you should use job boards as a way to build social capital. If you see an interesting position posted on the site, learn more about the company, and use your social capital to try to make a connection there.

Remember, you are no more than 6 degrees separated from any person on earth. The likelihood of you knowing someone who knows someone who is acquainted with someone at that company is great. Once you identify someone, reach out using your YOUTRY statement, it is just that simple.

Let's put in a little work.

I want you to research 12 common job boards and 12 specialized job boards and add them to the chart on the next page. Then, speak to your OGs and friends about the job sites that they may have used and found effective. If the ones used by others are not on your list, add them.

Take a picture of your list and share it with friends and family on social media using ***#makinitnation***.

Specialized Boards	Common Boards
1.	
2.	
3.	
4.	
5.	
6.	
7.	
8.	
9.	
10.	
11.	
12.	

Tapping Employment Agencies

Now, let's look at employment agencies.

Employment agencies will help you find a job. Usually, they have strong connections to employers and use those connections to help you succeed in getting a job. Basically, an agency serves as the middleman between the employer and you.

If you are thinking about using an agency, I need to be clear about one thing – they operate to meet the demands of business, **not yours**.

Yes, you need a job, but agencies' first concern is whether you are a good fit for the business. Without doing so, agencies run the risk of sending an employer someone who will not work out, eventually costing the employer more money in hiring, training, and lost productivity.

There are many types of employment agencies. Some are private and some are public. The private agencies fall under two categories: *personnel placement services* and *temporary help services*.

You must be careful, sometimes placement agencies try to charge you a fee. Don't sign up for one that does and make sure you ask if they charge any fees as soon as you walk into the door.

Personnel placement services usually contract with the employer to find qualified employees. That means the company that's hiring you is the one that pays the bill. That's why they are looking for the best. If you want to make personal placement services work for you then you must convince them that you are on top of your game. Apply many of the things that you learned in this guide. Build social capital with people who work there. Let them see the effort that you are putting into your own self-development and I guarantee, you will be hired in no time.

Temporary help services usually called staffing agencies are a good place to go when you need to find immediate work. The jobs are usually part-time with limited benefits and are often seasonal and temporary. When you need to make a quick buck or are looking for a part-time job to supplement your full-time income, then temp agencies can be a good bet. Many people turn temporary assignments into full-time jobs. It's a great way to get your foot in the door at some companies that you normally could not access. Once you get in, you let your social capital building powers do their thing.

If you are a college student, your school likely has a placement agency. Make sure you visit your placement office consistently and build social capital with the people there. If you are a high school student, your counselor should have a lot of information about jobs and local employers in the community. But the same rules apply - they are not going to send you to an employer just because you need a job. They are going to send you because you are ready for a job. So, you need to make sure you are ready and serious about holding down a job.

The other agency is a **workforce agency.** All of their services are free and they offer a range of training, education, and credentialing options. Workforce agencies can even help you get an apprenticeship. Apprenticeships are paid jobs where you learn a skill under the supervision of a skilled tradesperson. It combines classroom and hands-on learning to give you a good skillset and work experience that will lead to a good-paying career. Workforce centers also offer temporary certificate programs where you can get an industry-recognized credential, often in less than one year. These credentials can lead to a career-tracked job and some good money in your pocket.

Spending Your Thirty-Five

Now that we took a look at agencies, let's talk about how you plan to spend 17% of your 35 job hunting minutes each day – that's 6 minutes per day – to connect to an agency that can help you build the future that you seek. You could write up an email to reach out to an agency or connect with an OG who may have their own connections in an agency. Take a moment to brainstorm about how you can spend your 6 minutes each day. Write your ideas on the next page.

1. _____

_____

2. _____

_____

3. _____

_____

4. _____

_____

5. _____

_____

Direct Approach

Now for the final job search method, let's look at the **direct approach**.

The direct approach is often overlooked due to the limited number of people having the courage to do it. I think it is one of the most undervalued job search methods out there.

The direct approach means proactively reaching out to businesses and companies and letting them know that you are the right person for the job. It's that simple, but you gotta do it right.

Your best bet is to apply the technique that we taught you in this course. Once you identify the company, walk in and deliver your YOUTRY statement to the manager or supervisor. If you start with building social capital, getting the job will be easy. Turn that contact into a connect. Touch base with the person every month for three months informing them about the steps that you are taking to achieve workforce success. Before you know it, you'll not only have a job you will be helping others get jobs too.

So those are the four best job search methods (social capital, job boards, job Agencies, and direct approach). You are well on your way to job success, but we're missing something very important. In the next lesson, we'll take a look at how to build a simple yet powerful resume.

Building the Resume

To get you "job-ready" success certified; we'll need to look at a very important tool for success – your resume.

There is no one size fits all resume. As you go further in the world of work, your resume will adapt to your profession and position. While you may have heard of a resume, I want to take it one step further. We have developed an FEO RESUME. An FEO RESUME is an updated snapshot of one's FEO journey. Basically, we are looking at highlighting your Skills, Experience, Education, Connections, and Credentials.

I'm going to guide you through the resume creation process and then you'll complete an activity that will help you build one. If you already have a resume, I am sure you will still get something out of this section. Let's start by downloading the resume template now from *www.makinitnation.com*.

So, what should your resume entail?

1. Name & Contact Info

Yep, it's just that simple. Just make sure you know your full address -the way the post office has it marked! I've seen it all. Do not include any links to your social media pages or websites. And please use a simple email. If your email is outlandish like alldayhustling@yolo.com, it's time to get a simple, plain email. A good email address would be: **"first name.last name two favorite numbers @ gmail.com"**. Use the space below to write out your name and contact info as it should appear on your resume. Although there are many resume formats, this is the basic and it should provide you with a good start.

_____

_____

2. Summary

Think of the summary section like a souped-up YOUTRY statement. Although it is not required, I think it is an excellent way to add punch to your resume and get the reader interested in learning more about you. Basically, it should be a social capital-backed statement about who you are and why you are a great candidate for this position. Let's read a sample summary statement and then you'll do your own.

An industrious young man backed by workforce professionals who is committed to giving my best to improve productivity and maximize customer satisfaction.

What did you notice about our statement that is different from most entry-level and professional resumes? You probably noticed the social capital reference "-backed by workforce professionals." What is the first thing that you think of when you read this? You'll most likely wonder, "Who are these professionals?" It sparks an interest in the employer in who you know. Why? Because they are interested in expanding their social capital too and you may be one way of doing it. This is a very special technique that we only share with members of the MAKiN' iT Nation. Just make sure you have all your social capital assets lined up and ready. If you do the activities in this book, you will have that on lock.

Write up your summary below.

_____

_____

_____

_____

3. Experience

If you have little to no work experience to put on a resume, don't worry. We got you. In this section, we are going to focus on any experience that you have related to the position. Say, for example, that you are applying for a customer service position at a major cellular operator. Your experience section may look something like this:

Experience

Sales and Customer Service

Bronx, NY

- Helped local community organizations conduct outreach campaigns to promote the importance of education and work to youth in a summer leadership program.

- Developed promotional material for a startup entrepreneurial venture utilizing various social media channels.

- Sold a friend on the advantages of iOS over Android and secured another happy Apple customer.

- Helped a family member through cancer treatment by conducting routine tasks, assisting with personal care, and managing medication. She is doing well.

- Completed an online training course on workforce success.

Now you try. Brainstorm any experience that you have that relates to the position that you are interested in and document it creatively. Use one of your OGs as a sounding board.

_____

_____

_____

4. Education

Unless you have many degrees, this section will be short. If you are a high school student, whether you graduated or not, just list the school name, state, and the years attended. If you graduated, add the year of graduation.

For example, **Portland City High School, Portland, Oregon (2014-2019)**

Do the same if you are enrolled in a program. List the program name, state, and year(s) attended. If you completed the program, list the certificate or credential obtained.

If you have a credential that you earned directly from an association, list the granting organization, city, state, and the name of the credential and the year that it was obtained.

Fill out this section below.

_____

_____

_____

_____

5. Skills

Underneath education, you will list your skills. In this section, you will include any specific essential skills such as using a piece of equipment, software, social media channel, language, or special training. This list highlights your abilities that employers may find valuable. List your skills below.

1. _____

2. _____

3. _____

4. _____

5. _____

6. Awards and Activities

This is the final section of your resume. It allows you to list any clubs, sports, or community activities you've participated in that an employer may identify with. If you play chess, mention it. You never know if this will serve as a connection point with a future employer. Add a few here.

1. _____

2. _____

3. _____

4. _____

5. _____

Go back over each section and use what you wrote to compile your resume.

Make sure you spend some time with an OG looking over your final resume before getting it printed.

Cover Letter

A cover letter is like a partner to your resume. It is a way to get the employer to want to do more than call you in for an interview – it's going to make sure that they want to know you. With a well-written cover letter, you can present yourself to a prospective employer when you don't have the chance to wow them with your social capital building skills in person.

There are many websites on the internet that provide instructions on how to write a cover letter and provide samples that you can follow. You'll find a few in the resources section. However, most cover letters are not built on a social capital framework. We can make a few adjustments to the traditional cover letter design that will give it more a punch. We need to make your cover letter more than just an online application.

This is how.

A cover letter and a resume are nothing more than a fancy online application and have very little chance of getting you in the door. What gets you in the door is a connection. If you start your cover letter with the mention of a connection, you exponentially increase your chances of getting an interview, even possibly a job. Here's how you do it.

First, let's take a look at this sample letter:

Dear Charles Jones:

I am responding to the employment opportunity listed on your website. Please accept this letter and accompanying resume as evidence of my interest in applying for this job. I feel my qualifications and my skills would prove to be an asset to your organization.

Now let's give it the social capital twist.

Dear Charles Jones,

I am responding to the employment opportunity listed on your website. I was informed by Mr. Johnson, the head of the Baltimore Urban League that I could bring a lot of value to this position. Please accept this letter and accompanying resume as evidence of my interest in applying for this job. I feel my qualifications and my skills would prove to be an asset to your organization.

Notice that we mentioned Mr. Johnson and his title - the head of your local Urban League. What do you think the employer will think when reading this? The employer will be more interested in meeting you because they may be interested in who you now. Plus, it is a way to name your OGs in the application process. You should inform all your OGs that you are actively looking for a job and that you may use them as a reference. Just make sure you have their contact information handy, so you are not stumped during the interview when you are asked for it. Use the following template to draft your cover letter. Share your completed cover letters with your OGs to review before submission.

Application

Let's move on to the next step in the job hunt process – completing the application. An application is an official, legal form that employers ask all applicants to fill out in-person or online before being interviewed for a job. The application requests information about job seekers' employment history, educational background, degrees, qualifications, references, and more.

When filling out an application, it is a good idea to have your resume on hand. This way you can make sure that you're including the correct dates of employment, job titles, and education. Also, make sure to have on hand the names and contact information of your references. Let's go through some key points of filling out a job application.

If applying in person...

❖ **Bring a pen**

❖ **Turn off your cell phone**

❖ **Ask for two copies of the application** *(In case of errors on the first copy, you'll have another application ready)*

❖ **Read the application carefully and know what is being asked before filling anything out.**

❖ **Complete the application. If something doesn't apply to you, write "N/A"**

❖ **Check your answers for correct spelling, grammar, punctuation, completeness, and accuracy**

- ❖ If the application asks for the position desired, write in a specific position. Use the word "open" sparingly

- ❖ Salary expected: write negotiable. Even if you know the salary you want, make sure you keep room open to negotiate higher, if possible

- ❖ Make sure that you leave a good phone number, not one that will be cut off in a few weeks *(Before-hand, ask a responsible older relative or one of your OGs if they would receive an employment call on your behalf just in-case you aren't available. It will show employers the power of your social capital connections. If you don't have a reliable phone, other options include setting up a google voice account but make sure that you keep it professional. No wild greetings. As for email, no wild email names. Keep it simple.)*

- ❖ Be ready to explain any gaps in your work or education histories if you have any

- ❖ When asked "reason for leaving" in reference to your last job, never be negative. Use answers such as "school conflict," "conflicting hours," or "personal responsibilities." *(If you were fired from a job, you will be able to explain the circumstances during the interview.)*

Download the sample application and complete it. Once you're finished, have an OG look it over for comments. Once you receive their comments, complete another version with all the corrections. You may want to take a picture of your application so you can retrieve it when completing a real application.

Social Media Dangers

It's time for us to get into a very serious subject.

Is your social media presence contributing to economic suicide? 91% of companies will use social media to research you, and 69% admitted to not hiring candidates because of what appeared on their social media pages.

Let me ask you a question, and I want another honest answer. ***Is your Instagram account destroying your chances of getting a job?*** Let's examine the facts about social media and the role it can play in enhancing or destroying your connecting opportunities. Then, let's plan to ensure that you are not adversely affected. We call it ***"prep your rep."***

It's impossible to discuss the benefits of social media without first discussing the negatives. Corporations are using social media to vet potential employees. We have all heard social media horror stories. No one is immune. Stories abound about misplaced pictures, tweets, and inappropriate posts. It seems to spread more quickly than COVID-19. You should use social media responsibly; despite the fun it brings.

Most people think that they are safe behind their privacy settings. While most legitimate social media outlets have established privacy settings to protect the information you share and who has access to it, those **settings are not infallible**.

Social media is a billion-dollar industry. Money is made based on information about where people shop, what they buy, and how much they spend. Companies are looking to save millions of dollars on employee recruiting costs. An increasing number of companies are turning to social media for help in finding the right candidate.

Employers don't do the dirty work themselves. Due to the hidden dangers and legal implications of social media recruitment, many companies are safeguarding their interests by using third-party vendors. These third-party vendors may use unscrupulous tactics in getting past privacy settings to uncover unsettling information about you. There are already tons of applications and algorithms working to track every one of your postings, purchases, and downloads. Getting information about you is easy.

For your own good, I recommend *creating specific social media accounts until the job-search process is completed.* You may want to delete or suspend your other social media accounts, at least until the job, scholarship, or raise is secured. We could spend the rest of the book showing you how to set proper privacy settings, but by the time you complete this guide, those suggestions will already be outdated.

A major part of prepping your rep is to audit your social media presence and keep your online and social media appearances safe.

If you don't believe me, just think about this; a few years back, Suicide Squad and Guardians of the Galaxy director James Gunn was doing his thing as a big-name director, raking in billions of dollars in ticket sales. Seemingly out of nowhere, someone decided to repost some of his old tweets from almost a decade ago. These tweets were considered "insensitive" and they caused Disney to fire Gunn as director for the third installment of Guardians of Galaxy. These tweets were almost 10 years old! But that did not matter and it was enough to ruin his career.

Needless to say, your social media presence will MOST DEFINITELY have an impact on your career, so do yourself a favor and keep it clean.

A survey from CareerBuilder reports that hiring managers found that the following information contained in an applicant's social-media pages positively influenced their hiring decisions:

- ❖ evidence of a good personality

- ❖ professional image

- ❖ background information

- ❖ range of interests

- ❖ communication skills

- ❖ creativity

- ❖ references

Conversely, hiring managers stated that the following items were reasons not to hire a candidate:

- ❖ provocative/inappropriate photos/info

- ❖ drinking or using drugs

- ❖ poor communication skills

- ❖ bad-mouthing of previous employer

- ❖ discriminatory comments related to race, gender, religion, and so on

- ❖ lied about qualifications

The strategy is to make sure your social media works for you. So, what if you have to take down a site or two? Your friends will understand when they see you with a job or scholarship. Go through your profiles and see if they meet the qualifications based on the CareerBuilder survey.

Interview Skills

The **12x12x6 formula** should prepare you for the initial contact; let's talk about what to use to help you master answering those interview questions. My personal recommendation - use your social capital connections.

Think about it. You need reasons to stay connected to your social capital assets – your OGs. What better way than to call them up and ask them if they have ten minutes to help you with work on some interview questions. You will be reaffirming in their minds the fact that you are an eager and hardworking job seeker. Plus, your OGs have been through interviews many times. It is so much easier to learn from others than from a book. Also, they might share some information about available job opportunities.

Looking the Part

To be a success you need to look like success. Dressing to impress is not what we are talking about. Wearing clothes that suit the role you're showing up for goes a long way in getting ahead. Times are evolving; a nose ring or tattoo no longer negates your employability, but it will limit it.

Yes, you are your own brand but if you want to work for another brand – you need to be ready to do some code-switching. How neatly and professionally you present yourself determines if you'll land the job and be valued as someone employers are interested in investing in.

Brush your teeth and wash your face every morning before going in, and make sure your hair and clothes are clean and smell fresh. Avoid body odor, but at the same time, make sure you're not doused in body spray or perfume; strong scents can be just as detracting from your professional appearance as bad body odor.

Always keep your appearance neat. Don't ever wear pants with holes in them, and shirts with offensive or crude slogans. Moreover, make sure your clothes are practical for the job. If you aren't sure about the best look, button-downs, sweaters, and blouses are all easy ways to look sharp.

Nowadays there is a huge intersection where 'professional' and 'fashionable' meet. Just keep things sharp, and avoid clothes that show your belly or underwear, or clothes you bought to party, exercise, or lounge around the house binging Netflix in. Avoid tight-fitting clothing and, if you are a male, make sure that you always wear socks.

It boils down to staying smart. If you're at a loss, a button-down paired with pants or a skirt is never the wrong choice. If you're in a job or program that has uniforms, consider yourself lucky! All you have to remember is to keep up with your personal hygiene and make sure you always have a clean uniform, so you never find yourself in a bind on the morning of a shift.

So how do you stack up in your appearance? Are you ready for that job?

Answer each question below using "N" for Never, "S" for Sometimes, and "A" for Always, depending on how well you take care of your appearance every day.

1. **Do I keep my body clean?** _____

2. **Do I take a frequent shower or bath?** _____

3. **Do I clean and trim my nails?** _____

4. **Do I use a deodorant?** _____

5. **Is my hair neat and combed in private?** _____

6. **Is my hair washed weekly or more often?** _____

7. Do I brush my teeth daily? _____

8. Do I visit the dentist every 6 months? _____

9. Do I have a yearly medical check-up? _____

10. Do I eat a balanced diet? _____

11. Do I stand and sit straight? _____

12. Are my clothes neat, clean, and mended? _____

13. Are my shoes clean and polished? _____

14. Do I dress right for the event? _____

15. Most importantly, do I like myself? _____

In two sentences, how would you sum up your own personal style and appearance?

_____

_____

_____

What changes, if any, would you make to your own appearance? What is a change you can take on now?

_____

_____

_____

_____

Speak to an OG and get their dress recommendations. If you are smooth, they may even help you get your hands on some official dress for workforce success. Check out our resource section for tons of information on how to dress appropriately for the world of work.

Job Hunting Smarts

Ask anyone in the job-hunting game, and they'll be quick to tell you that *applying to jobs is and should be a full-time job*. To make it – and nail those interviews – you must get the most out of your time. There's a big difference between working hard and working smart. By using our job hunt success formula, you will succeed.

It can be overwhelming to wake up in the morning and see "get a job" on your to-do list. When you give yourself such an open-ended task, it feels impossible to know where to start. But if you break that mountain-sized task into smaller pieces, it goes from feeling impossible to looking manageable.

Follow the path of thousands of successful people before you to avoid the trap of too-large tasks: make a schedule. All successful people have a schedule they follow, whether they're your biology teacher or Beyoncé. That's exactly what you need to do as you hunt for the right job to help you build up your FEO.

Instead of having a to-do list that just says, "get a job," think about seven tasks you can complete today to work toward that goal. **Think achievable**. Maybe one task is simply writing a list of places to apply. Another task can be finding one volunteer opportunity within walking distance. Get started now!

Fill out at least ten things to do and the times you'll do them to maximize the hours in your day. When you build your schedule, remember to include any appointments or plans you've already made, so you aren't caught off guard tomorrow. Tomorrow morning don't hesitate. Follow this schedule and see what happens. By working smart, you'll be unlocking the potential for your goals to bear that fruit.

Task	Date & Time
1.	
2.	
3.	
4.	
5.	
6.	
7.	
8.	
9.	
10.	

Great Job. You are well on your way. You are putting in hard work. Congratulations! Let's keep pushing.

OGs Shared Knowledge

In this chapter, I created my resume and cover letter and shared it with one of my OGs, _____.

We discussed:

_____

_____

My OG suggested:

_____

_____

I also asked my OG to help me to practice answering interview questions. *(Describe the conversation)*

_____

_____

_____

They suggested:

_____

_____

I learned:

_____

_____

I'll keep them updated every _____ on my progress.

Date completed: _____

CHAPTER 7

I want you to remember that ___a job is more than just a chance to earn some money.___ I know we've discussed this several times in the earlier chapters, but it's so important that you never forget this fact. A job is a building block for your future. The ages of 14-26 **ARE NOT** your wealth-building years, these are your Future Economic Opportunity years, your FEO.

Getting an education, securing credentials, building social capital, learning skills, and getting work experience are the most important things that you can do to reach long term success. That's why during your FEO years, you are building the foundation for economic success.

Think about it – the sooner you start building the foundation, the quicker you can get the house built.

There are five components of FEO. You can think of them like four walls and a roof of your foundation. You'll have to build up each piece one by one, but once you've finished, you'll have a solid foundation to house your opportunities where they'll grow into economic success.

Work Experience

The most obvious perk of working is the experience. Getting work experience under your belt is the key to landing better-paying jobs. Plus, you need to have something to put on a job application and a resume.

Let's be clear though, ***just showing up is not work experience***.

Work experience is a documented history of job attendance, punctuality, and responsibilities. Some of us know people who had a job but couldn't use it as work experience because they got fired, quit, or had problems with the boss. That's just wasted time and energy that led to nothing worthwhile.

It's not just clocking in that'll pave the way for success. You have to put the effort in, learn the tasks, and be an employee that your supervisor will be happy to vouch for in the future.

Don't blow your work experience by quitting on a dime or getting fired because you didn't do your job. Keep a record of the new skills you learn.

In the MAKiN' iT nation, we are training to build two new skills every sixty-six days. That could be communication skills and public speaking skills or team cooperation skills and time management skills. I want you to take part in this challenge. Use your S.M.A.R.T Skills template to choose new skills to learn and put them into action. Let your OG know what you're up to so they can provide you with some accountability.

If you're continually showing up for work on time with these new skills, you'll have the work experience on lock in no time.

Let me hook you up with an easy way to make sure that you're gaining actual work experience and not just working.

Step 1: *Ask!* Approach your supervisor or seasoned co-worker and get their recommendations on making the most of your work experience. If you haven't started work yet, be sure to ask them for this advice during your first week.

Step 2: When you get the job, *constantly reflect on your work experience*. Even if you are not enjoying it, it doesn't mean it is a waste of time. Think about the things you are learning, the social capital that you are developing, and how both could help you in getting a better job.

Step 3: *Get involved.* Find out if other things are going on in the company. Are there opportunities to volunteer or mentor? Some companies even offer training courses specifically designed to help you move up to a higher position. These things will help you find meaning. As we learned earlier, work satisfaction is all about meaning.

Step 4: *Job-shadow others.* Gain a better understanding of the work of other departments by job-shadowing. Learn about opportunities throughout your company, the skills required for the positions, and their typical job duties. Build social capital during this process. It will show everyone at the company that you are a go-getter and hungry for more opportunities.

Step 5: *Set objectives*. Know exactly what you want to gain from your work experience opportunity. Use the S.M.A.R.T method to develop these objectives. As an employee with a plan, management will know that you are serious about work and possibly fast track you for management or a better paying position.

Step 6: *Actively work on the supervisor's suggestions.* If your supervisor tells you to make sure that you are on-time, research things that you can do to make this happen. If your supervisor says, make customers feel more welcomed, explore strategies that'll help you become the type of employee your supervisor needs you to be.

Next time you go to work, or whenever you start working, put these steps into action immediately, and soon you'll have your first wall built.

Social Capital

Remember this: *social capital leads to references but references don't lead to social capital.*

When you get to work, I want you to take a good look at the co-workers and supervisors around you. These are the people who could influence your career. For better or worse, the connections you make now can lead to opportunities in the future. So you gotta ***play the game right***.

Let's take Carla, for example.

> Carla just got a job as a housekeeper at a hotel. In just a few months, she has built social capital with various co-workers including Jasmine, a receptionist who's been working there for over 10 years. In a series of conversations, Carla expressed to Jasmine how much she enjoys interacting with customers and her admiration for how the hotel is run. Jasmine has seen how great of an employee Carla is; she shows up on time and goes

above and beyond work expectations. Jasmine decides to speak to the manager about considering Carla for the newly open concierge position, a position that pays almost double her current wage. After just one short interview, Carla is given the position.

Now imagine if Carla didn't care about how she was viewed at work, didn't care about building social capital, and only showed up to get a paycheck.

For the sake of your future, don't make a bad impression. By showing up to work with a stink face and a salty attitude, clocking in late, or being rude to customers, you're negatively impacting your future career chances.

Failing to make an impression at all is even worse. This is a less talked about mistake that most young people make at their first job. Don't invest your energy in staying under the radar and scraping by doing only what's been asked. By doing the bare minimum, you're missing out on the opportunity to build social capital. Connect with those around you because you never know who can help you open doors. *Play chess, not checkers.*

Social capital leads to references but references don't lead to social capital.

You got to work at building social capital. Getting a reference is easy. Every job you apply for will ask for references. Your job supervisor and co-workers will provide them. They can help you navigate new jobs down the road. If you've proven yourself as a reliable person, they will most likely support you in any endeavor. They might even try to take you with them when they get a new job.

It's easy to go from being a forgettable employee (or a downright bad one) to a knockout one.

How?

Just ask those who've been successful at their job. Success leaves clues. Ask them to tell you everything they can about their experiences on the job. You'll be amazed by the insight and wisdom others possess.

Remember to be kind and open. Smile. Take a genuine interest in listening to what people have to say and build a human connection. **Nothing feels worse than talking**

to someone who's only half-listening. Put away your phone. Let me say that again **– put away your phone!**

As soon as you get a job or meet someone who works at a job you want, ask about how to succeed at that company. Let's review some questions that you can ask:

- ❖ What's the most important thing that you've learned since working here?

- ❖ What was the hardest thing for you starting out?

- ❖ What do you wish someone had told you your first month here?

- ❖ What is your favorite and least favorite thing about the job?

- ❖ Any advice for me on how to grow in my position?

When they give you answers, don't let it just go in one ear and out the other. Actually use the advice they've given you and implement them in daily work life.

Credentials

As you know from chapter four, credentials are a crucial aspect of getting paid. With an industry-backed credential that you can earn in less than two years, you can be on your way to a good-paying career with a lot of room for growth and advancement. Having a job is the best way to learn about credentials. Use your supervisors and co-workers to learn about the in-demand credentials needed for your industry or occupation. Get their recommendations for reputable programs where you can get credentials for what interests you.

If you are a hard worker, don't be afraid to ask about opportunities in which the company could sponsor your credential. People often don't know what it is you want, but once you open up and tell them, they'd be more than happy to help you get there.

Education

Getting your high school diploma is crucial if you want to get ahead in life. However, you do have a choice about what to do after high school. College is not for everyone, at least not right away. So as an alternative, you may want to consider two-year programs. Maybe give some real, creative thought about your passions. Curious about physical therapy? Start looking into online and short-term training programs. Want to be a graphic artist? Explore what your community college has to offer. Ask for placement at an art studio or a recreation center where you can put your interests to work.

The possibilities are endless as long as you're looking for them. As always, start with your OGs. Ask them about the paths they took regarding education and work after high school.

Here are a few questions to get you started:

❖ How did education help you get to where you are?

❖ What were the benefits of post-high school education?

❖ What type of educational program did you pursue?

❖ What were the costs?

❖ What do you wish you had known when you were starting out?

Education is the fourth and final wall in your foundation. All you need now is a roof to top it all off.

Skills

No matter what job you land, you can learn valuable skills while working.

Yet, we often have the wrong idea when we think of skills. When we talk about skills, our minds frequently jump to things like how to use a certain tool or a computer program. Those are only half the types of skills you can learn – those are called **"hard skills."**

"Soft skills", on the other hand, are interpersonal qualities better known as *"people skills."* These are things like work ethic, communication, time management, and problem-solving.

Soft skills are all about your ability to be a team player, keep a positive attitude, work well under pressure, and manage constructive criticism. Often, soft skills are written off as personality traits (and therefore unlearnable), but soft skills, in truth, are things you have the power to master, like any other skill.

Regardless of the job you are looking for, ***soft and hard skills are a must***. Employers aren't just looking for one or the other – that's why we refer to these as **essential skills**. They are looking at the whole package. If you want to stand out from the pack, you must work on developing these essential skills.

A good method is The MAKiN' iT **2/1/66 rule**: learn two new skills and build one new habit every sixty days. If you put this rule into effect every two months, you will see major improvements in your life. In one year, you will have ten new skills and six new habits. That, my friend, is how to **MAKE IT!**

Let's do a cool exercise to get started off with the right set of skills. I want you to send a message to all of your OGs asking them:

What's the number one skill that I should learn in order to be successful and how should I learn it?

Their answers should be as diverse as our fingerprints.

You now have a solid foundation that you can use to accomplish your financial goals. Four walls and a roof is all you need to get started. So use this foundation to start pushing forward and go hard after the future you desire.

OG's Shared Knowledge

This chapter was all about getting advice and information from OGs and coworkers. At work, I asked my coworker _____ about our workplace and how they felt about it. They told me:

_____

_____

_____

I also asked them if they knew of any credential opportunities. They said:

_____

_____

I am going to use the information to propel me forward by:

_____

_____

I talked to OG _____ about their education experience and if they had any advice for me. They suggested:

_____

_____

I am going to apply this knowledge to my life by:

_____

_____

I'll keep them updated on my progress every _____.

Date completed: _____

CHAPTER 8

So far, you've been putting in serious work. You should be extremely proud of yourself! I know that applying all of this information to your daily life isn't easy. Throughout this whole process, you have been reshaping your mind and your life and that's no easy task. But I guarantee that it will pay off in ways that you may have never dreamed possible. So, let's keep pushing forward and soon you'll reach the ultimate goal of economic success.

In this chapter, we are going to look beyond how to make money and take a look at what to do with the money you make.

Don't get me wrong, it is absolutely true that "a job is more valuable than a paycheck." However, a paycheck does come with a job and you need to know what to do with it once it gets deposited into your bank account.

Paychecks have a funny way of slipping through fingers. Your bank account balance can turn to zero in a hot second and you won't have an idea about where your money went. You'll think someone stole directly out of your bank account. To add insult to injury, bank charges will throw your account in the red and you'll wind up losing more than you made. And **the more money you make; the harder it is to keep track of it.**

When you're a kid, per week you are used to making money in the tens - $40, $80, $90. When you become a teen, you start earning in the low hundreds - $200, $300, and as a young adult, you get into the high hundreds - $500, $700.

Whether it's $8 or $15 an hour, just remember, Uncle Sam is going to get his cut but you will still have a five-digit bank account balance staring at you – the question is *what are you going to do with it?*

Let's look at ways to keep the money you make.

If you're following the rules in this guide, then you are preparing for bigger paychecks down the road. And the best way to prepare for bigger paychecks tomorrow is by building better money habits today.

Soon you will have legitimate cash flow – and with legitimate cash flow, you can make some major moves. But when you're just starting out, you get excited about the amount you're earning and you blow it. We took a youth survey to see what type of things young money makers blew their first paycheck on.

Here are the top 10:

1. Booze or drugs

2. Sneaker game

3. Take out

4. Fashion brands

5. Tattoos

6. Lotto tickets/Scratch-offs

7. Boyfriend/Girlfriend/Other

8. Concerts

9. Video games

10. Weed

Did you or anyone you know blow their check on any of these items?

Even professional athletes fall victim to "balling too hard." Ball player Antoine Walker was one of them. Growing up in the South Side of Chicago, Walker didn't come from money. So, when he made it into the league and started earning tens of millions of dollars each season, he began spending non-stop. He bought two Bentleys, two Mercedes, a Range Rover, a Cadillac Escalade and a Hummer. By the end of his career, he spent or gave away of his money and eventually filed for bankruptcy.

I get it. When you get money, you can't help but to want to flex. It's tempting to blow it on things that you don't really need.

It all goes back to the survival scale.

Many people live with an immediate results mindset, where they place more weight on present rewards than those in the future.

For example, let's say your future self wants to buy a home, but your present self wants to splurge on new Jordans – which one will you choose?

Every time you let the immediate results mindset win; you are training your brain to value immediate gratification over longer-term interests. In this case, you will likely have the coolest looking sneakers but not a home to call your own.

By saving more of what you earn and continuing to be mindful of where that money's going, you're setting yourself up for more cash flow in the future. And if you manage your cash flow properly, you will be able to manage your bills and enjoy the life you want.

Let's go through a few activities to help you learn how to make some good cashflow moves.

An Honest Budget

If you don't know how to control cash flow, cash flow will control you. An out of control cashflow turns into no cashflow real quick. Look at people who landed a record deal, modeling contract, or pro ball position. They think that they are set for life … then money mismanagement happens. Twenty years later – they are broke. Let's be careful so that we don't wind up like them and start learning how to be smart with the money we make.

Take a look at the sample monthly budget on the next page.

Income	Expenses
Paycheck - $1,365	Rent - $800
Lyft Income - $573	Gas (for car) - $50
Allowance - $55	Light Bill - $65
	Gas Bill (for house) - $50
	Water Bill - $40
	Groceries - $200
	Phone Bill - $100

Let's start with the income side.

Your income comes from the money you earn on a regular, consistent basis during a particular month (wages, allowance, part-time legal hustles, rental income, etc.) Your income can change from month to month so make sure to adjust your budget for that month's scheduled earnings.

Underneath income is where we track expenses - the things that you NEED to spend money on during a month. Like income, expenses can change so make sure that you adjust your budget each month. Remember *expenses are NEEDS, not WANTS.* Expenses are things that you need to function day to day like housing, food, transportation, lunch, clothing, utility bills, cell phone, gas, investing, and emergencies. Feel free to add in whatever else that you think you'll NEED. If some items are covered by a parent or guardian, leave it blank. Just understand that you'll be responsible for those items one day.

Now you may be saying, "What about the things I WANT?"

I hear you. There is a simple formula to take care of your NEEDS and WANTS – we call is the 70/10/20 formula - 70% of your income goes to your needs, 10% towards savings and investments, and the other 20% goes towards any form of "WANT" that you may have.

What happens if 70% does not cover your needs? This happens often but the solution is simple. You'll either need to make more money or cut back on some of those WANTS.

You may want that apartment but you can't afford the rent so you might have to take in a roommate. You may want that car, but you can't afford the payment, so keep saving and buy a car with cash. Taking the bus for a few more months won't kill you.

Sticking with this formula is a smart move, one that I hope you are ready to make.

It's mandatory to put 10% of whatever you make away for savings. Savings are key. If you make $300 a week, the minimum amount that you should put away is $30. Savings will allow you to handle emergencies when they arise and you know they will.

According to analysts at Bankrate, the average emergency costs over $1000. So, if you're saving $30 a week, you would have to save for 33 weeks to save $1000. So, get started as soon as you get your first paycheck.

Once you have over a G stacked for emergencies, start thinking about making some investments. The best investment that you can make is staying out of debt. So, save more so you can always buy things with cash. Credit will ruin you faster than a bad haircut.

Go ahead and fill in your sample budget.

Income	Expenses

If you don't have a job use the income of $250 a week which is $1000 a month and see what you come up with. If your expenses exceed your income, you are going to have to cut back on expenses or increase your income. When the two equal each other, that's what we call a **balanced budget**.

Also, speak to a few OGs for budgeting tips and information about part-time legal side hustles. Just about everyone has one. When I'm not creating courses or traveling around the country speaking to young people and educators, I'm selling my old stuff on the internet. It's fun and I am able to make some extra cash.

Next up, we will look at the secret to getting money in the workplace.

Productivity

Showing up to work just to earn a paycheck is not the recipe for success. A company of unproductive workers is a company that's doomed to fail. In fact, there is an epidemic of unproductive workers out there.

Let's be honest, texting friends is not work!

Looking at social media is not work.

Taking extended breaks is not work.

How many hours of NOT working do you think the average employee puts in each day?

Research states that out of an 8-hour workday the average worker puts in 5 hours on "NOT WORK." Is that crazy or what?

That means that the average worker only works 3 hours a day out of an 8-hour shift. No wonder it is so easy to get ahead at work, you just got to put in work!

That's what I've been trying to teach you since the start of the course.

**Hard work beats talent, especially when talent does not want to work hard.**

You may be wondering why you should care about costing an employer a few dollars. After all, you're still getting yours. If you're in a subsidized job, you may even feel like it's not even the company that's paying you – it's Uncle Sam.

But not so fast. Companies still face tons of costs for hiring you no matter who cuts your check. These are called **indirect costs** – the cost of having someone supervise you; the cost of resources so you can do the job right and the cost of working space so that you can actually do your job.

Indirect costs can result in companies losing thousands of dollars for each unproductive employee. And it hurts you just as much as it hurts them with the loss of connections, promotions, references, and the opportunity to learn a skill or secure a credential.

If you're in an unsubsidized job, then your poor work ethic directly impacts your employers financially. If you are not being productive, doing what you're supposed to and more, that lack of drive will impact your company's cash flow, and if the company heads can't pay themselves, they certainly will not pay you.

If you're breaking into the tip-based industry – think servers, bartenders, baristas, and performers – your customers will notice if you're on your phone, ignoring them, and not valuing their time, and they will tip you accordingly.

If you fail to show up on time, complete tasks, and be an employee worth hiring, you will be fired and completely lose your cash flow as well as the opportunity to build FEO. Strolling in late after going to lunch or taking a sick day to head to the movies, will put you on the chopping block.

If you come across as an employee who costs more than they contribute, you could be spoiling opportunities for other young people down the line.

Don't be the reason others lose out on an opportunity, be the reason why they get it.

The easiest way to be a productive employee is to work when you say you will. Show up when you're scheduled. Do your tasks and ask for something else to do when you're finished. Give your best self every single day. When the work is done, instead of hanging out with your friends and sharing a cigarette out back, find your supervisor and ask what else can be done. Organize the work van or wipe down counters. Put things away. Read the manual.

By being a driven and motivated employee, you will have cash flow and you will be setting up the stage to have more cash flow in the future.

These small changes will revolutionize your future because while everyone else is proving to their employers that they are unproductive working only 5 out of 8 hours a day, you're greatly outshining them. Getting ahead is simple. Just work.

When you are an employee worth noticing, you are inviting raises, long-term employment opportunities, and other benefits. By giving a position your all, you quickly learn the ins and outs, discover your favorite and least favorite aspects, and are better equipped to shift into a position that aligns with what you love.

How much does unproductivity actually cost?

Let's say that a fast-food worker spends 5 minutes on her phone when she should be working.

If her hourly wage is $10.00 per hour or 16 cents per minute, she is costing the employer 85 cents every hour by being unproductive.

If we look at the cost for a year, the total cost to the employer would be $1,216.67 per year.

That's enough for four average car payments!

This is only an example but imagine if this was a true situation. It is clear that unproductivity is damaging both to the employee and the employer.

Leaving Work

By embracing a workforce success mindset and a dedication to productivity, you'll be building a lot of future economic opportunities.

But beware: when you're productive, an employer may want you to work more and may offer you all sorts of promotions, perks, and increases in pay to stay onboard. After all, with the average worker putting in only 3 hours of productivity during an 8-hour day, it would be crazy to ever let you go.

So, how do you balance it all out? You're bound to grow tired. You'll have more energy on some days and feel run down on others. So how do you balance it out so that you don't burn yourself out? I recommend that you **work no more than 20 hours a week.**

Research shows, working more than 20 hours a week can be a big hit to building your FEO. Why? The more you work, the less time you have for school and other forms of education. Let's face it, working two 8-hour shifts is going to make getting up for school or concentrating on that online class real difficult.

Working 20 or more hours per week can also increase the likelihood that you will drop out of school - high school or college. That doesn't make sense when the payoff for a high school diploma is $410,000 more with it than without it. A college degree earns you about $1 million more over your lifetime than just a high school diploma.

Work messes with your money and you need to be very careful about working extra hours in place of investing in the things that will bring you a real big paycheck down the line.

Another reason why working over 20 hours per week is not such a good idea is that it interferes with recreation, sports, and civic activities – the places where you can build tons of social capital.

Let me put it this way, at work you are probably stuck with a whole bunch of people who also earn $14 an hour. If you are stuck around $14 an hour wage earners, you run the risk of staying stuck as a $14 wage earner. You need to build social capital with others who are earning $35 an hour or more, so you can be a $35 an hour earner too. Joining sports teams, clubs, and doing volunteer work, are all excellent ways to build social capital and create a future beyond your wildest imagination.

The bottom line is if you are in the FEO years, ages 14 to 26, these are not your wealth-building years. These are the years you need to maximize each element of FEO so you can make it to your wealth-building years ready to rock. Wealth building years are from 27 to 55. During this time period, if you have your FEO on lock - your education completed, many skills mastered, social capital coming out of your ears, tight work experience, and a few credentials under your belt - how much do you see yourself making then?

So why make chump change now? In a few years, you will be able to amass a small fortune, but you need to make sure your working hours stay at or under 20 hours each week. Turn down the extra hours they offer, no matter how enticing quick money is, and invest those hours in your FEO future instead. If you feel you need to focus on your education or move on to a program that pushes your skill set further, don't be afraid to pass promotions or leave the job. Just leave the job the right way. Make sure you move forward with a reference in hand, at least two skills mastered, and a solid track record of attendance and reliability. If you are leaving or reducing hours because of school reasons – that's cool. Don't stress it. People leave jobs for many reasons. More than 3 million workers quit their jobs each month, that's approximately 3% of the US workforce.

Let's look at the proper way to leave a job because leaving the wrong way will most certainly come back to haunt you.

Here are some ways to leave a job properly.

First, if you have a problem with a boss or a co-worker, you should **always try to sort it**. Most companies have grievance procedures – follow them. This may not always solve the problem, but it is a step in the right direction.

Second, you should **never just walk off the job under any circumstance**. Make sure that you have another job lined up if you plan on walking out. Have you ever heard the phrase, "It's easier to find a job when you have a job?" Why does this seem true? There are a few simple answers. Unemployed job seekers may appear too eager to land a job. This could work against you. This over-excitement may draw negative attention from an employer. They may start to ask why is this candidate unemployed? Finding a job when you have a job also signals to an employer that you are not the type of person who gets fired simply because you still have a job. Employers know you are still well connected. Well-connected people get jobs faster than those who are not well connected. That may make the employer decide whether to hire you if they really want you on the team.

Third, give your supervisor at least two weeks' notice. Be calm and tell them that you decided to move on for personal reasons. Make sure you thank them for the opportunity in a heartfelt way. Also, be sure to tell your supervisor that you are leaving before anyone else does. You don't want your employer to find out that you've been gossiping about leaving. it's not a good look.

Another thing to do when leaving a job is to make sure you get some type of documentation about your job performance while you are still employed. Ask for a reference letter for school. Make sure that you always get official documentation about the type of employee that you are and the quality of the work that you did before you walk out the door.

Finally, be even more productive in your last two weeks than in your first two weeks. Offer to train your replacement. Showing concern and integrity will go a long way in helping you keep that company and your supervisor, as social capital assets.

It's simple! Employers favor the employed.

Remember that it is ok to leave work as long as work never leaves you.

OGs Shared Knowledge

In this chapter, I worked up my own budget plan and shared it with one

of my OGs, _____.

We talked about:

_____

_____

_____

_____

They also suggested:

_____

_____

_____

_____

With this knowledge, I am going to:

_____

_____

_____

_____

_____

I'll be sure to keep them updated on my progress every _____.

Date completed: _____

CHAPTER 9

So maybe by now you've landed a job or are at least in the final throes of getting one.

Congratulations!

Now it's time to start thinking about the best ways to be a stellar employee.

Consistently working on your FEO is hard work. Sometimes, you may feel drawn to the path of least resistance, falling into traps that give you a quick turnaround while putting your life, freedom, and FEO at risk.

I'll level with you: if being a success was easy, everyone would be jumping on board. The truth is ***success requires discipline, hard work, and a laser focus.*** To develop that single-mindedness, you must be motivated.

The big question is, where does that motivation come from?

Often, our society hones in on external motivators like peer pressure, wanting something fancy, or hoping to make your loved ones proud. But real motivation, the kind that lasts through all kinds of weather, comes from inside.

It's called **intrinsic motivation**. Intrinsically motivated people undertake an activity or job for its own sake, for the learning potential, or the feelings of accomplishment the work itself awakens.

In contrast, external factors are called **extrinsic motivation** and they push someone to do a task so they can get a reward or avoid a punishment separate from the activity itself – think money, new kicks, or bragging rights. The problem with extrinsic motivators is that they run out. The new kicks get scuffed, money drains to pay the bills, and soon your friends will all have jobs too.

Intrinsic motivations keep you going when the extrinsic ones lose their shine.

It's a curious thing, isn't it? Intrinsic and extrinsic motivations.

Why are some people more extrinsically motivated?

I want you to take a moment and think about someone in your life who may be intrinsically motivated. What do they do? Why do they do it?

Whatever that person has in their life that inspires them to be intrinsically motivated can be nurtured in your own life too. Maybe you need to pursue something that motivates you or work toward a broader goal in building your FEO.

Keeping Motivation Alive

Intrinsic motivation helps to keep you going when those extrinsic motivators are missing. Work isn't always glamorous. There won't always be someone reminding you to do something, or a looming punishment threatening you to work harder. By expecting external motivators to push you toward the right track (like a paycheck) you set yourself up for a line of disappointment. By moving through life as an extrinsically motivated individual, you may lose out on opportunities that might have otherwise changed your life.

Let's look at a technique that I like to do to keep myself intrinsically motivated. I use it when I'm feeling down or feel like giving up. I ask myself these questions and respond while looking in the mirror.

> **What will you lose if you don't get this done and how does that make you feel?**
>
> **If you keep on this track, where do you see yourself in five months?**
>
> **What if you were motivated to get it done, what do you gain? How would your life look, five months from now?**
>
> **What's one small thing that you can and will do right now?**
> *Then I go out and do it. *

The key is to choose something that you can do immediately - like read one paragraph, run one minute, answer an email, pay a bill. Put all of your energy into getting that one thing done. And you'll be surprised how much you'll get done.

Virtual Drainers

Having a healthy balance of internal and external motivation is the key to success.

Shifting your mentality to foster a healthy balance takes diligence, repetition, and practice. By participating in this course, and doing the exercises, you've taken vital steps in the work needed to motivate yourself. There are a million things you are capable of becoming just through motivation and a good attitude.

Sometimes it's hard to be motivated when many around you are not. And believe it or not, social media can have a huge impact on your ability to stay motivated.

If you spend a lot of time on social media and you find yourself lacking motivation, there is one way to change the game; ***stop subscribing to the negative influencers that keep you away from positive habits, the drive to acquire skills, or the full potential you have.***

These virtual drainers thrive on your lack of energy. Misery loves company and people hate to see you doing better than them. So, leave it alone and do your thing.

But social media doesn't have to be all bad. Sister Yo-Utu-Be (YOUTUBE) is usually always positive. She'll show you how to make it in any field out there. Think of the career you're most interested in and do a quick search on YouTube. In less than a second, you'll have a slew of positive videos of people being amazing at your dream job.

Communicate Effectively

A critical part of making it is being able to effectively communicate one-on-one and in group situations. A communicator knows how to think on their feet and maintain composure when the unexpected inevitably happens.

At work, you may find yourself overwhelmed by the overall rush of the workplace, people telling you what to do, customers asking you difficult questions. It may be an instant reaction to get salty or turn up your stink face but hold back for a minute. Try non-inflammatory communication and be smooth, letting your chill and positivity serve as pillars to how you handle these situations. Instead of rolling your eyes, opt for less aggressive and clear communication. Often, someone doesn't realize they're being rude. You never know if a person could simply be having a bad day.

The only way to avoid drama is to make sure you never start it in the first place.

I'll give it to you straight: you won't like everyone you ever meet – and not everyone you meet will like you. And that's okay. You don't have to be best friends with every coworker or change the life of each customer.

What you do need to do is exercise civility if you hope to translate your work experience to meaningful opportunity and income down the line. So instead of wondering how to get back at a coworker or assert dominance over a situation, show up as your best and most professional self, and you'll be sure to prevail in any situation thrown your way.

Avoid swearing or inflammatory language, regardless of how frustrated you may feel in a situation at work. In a professional setting, leave that language at the door; you never know who you'll offend, and it's better to avoid any drama altogether by keeping your language to the kind you'd use to talk to your grandmother.

Of course, none of your words matter if you spend the whole-time mumbling. Mumbling and rambling negate any important or intelligent thoughts you may be sharing with coworkers and can aggravate customers looking for information and assistance.

Speak up!

Project your voice as best you can by pushing air through your stomach to make sure your valuable input doesn't go unheard. You have smart and important things to say; don't let them get lost because you're too self-conscious to get loud.

LISTENING

Perhaps just as important as speaking up is knowing when to listen.

The trick to being a good listener is surprisingly easy: when someone else is talking, *don't plan what you're going to say next.* That's it. If you're listening to someone's story or idea and your wheels are spinning on how to share your own story, then you aren't listening – you're just looking for an audience to appreciate you. By opening your ears up to what others have to say, you're positioning yourself to make connections and learn things that may surprise you.

Think about it: what's the point of a conversation if you already know what you're going to say? You may as well be talking to the mirror if that's all you want. The purpose of conversing is to engage, learn, and exchange ideas. You'll be pleasantly surprised by everything there is to learn once you open yourself up to learning from others.

Here are a few tips to becoming a good listener:

1. **Make Consistent Eye Contact**
   I'm not talking about being a robot. You can blink but just don't go looking at everything except the person talking.

2. **Paraphrase**
   Paraphrasing is restating the speaker's thoughts in your own words. For instance, "let me get this right, you want me to..." Or, if you are dealing with an angry customer: "So, you're frustrated that your order wasn't correct, let me see what I can do to make it right." This technique is instrumental in resolving conflict and improving productivity. It shows others that you are professional and worthy of a raise.

3. **Nod and Smile**
   It's a great way to show you agree and want to hear more, as you don't have to interrupt the person who is talking.

4. **Listen to Understand**
   Possess a real desire to listen to another. Don't simply interject. Go a whole conversation without speaking and try to walk away with as many points as

you can. You are not learning when you speak. The person talking will feel your eagerness to learn.

want you to think of a person who demonstrates good listening skills and send hem a note thanking them for doing so. Below, write out how you can put these our listening skills to work immediately.

_____

_____

_____

_____

_____

Provider Service

On the other side of customer service, there's something called "**provider service.**" t refers to the attitude you hold towards the people providing you a service. If you .reat teachers, cashiers, counselors, security guards, and library attendants with espect, people notice just like they'll notice if you are rude.

Real wealth is treating other people well, regardless of which side of the exchange you're on. That respect will go a long way in having people help make things happen or you. In fact, organizations, not only individuals are a great source of social :apital.

What I have learned from my years helping young people succeed is that many organizations have been there to help. It is usually not one organization that helped. Young people have been part of many organizations. Sometimes the outcomes were good and sometimes not so much.

Let's take some time out to appreciate the organizations from our past. I want you o think about programs that you have been part of in the past and go online and secure their contact information. If there are new staff, that's fine. Otherwise, try to find someone who will remember you. If you can' t find someone, reach out to the Director.

Inform then that you were part of the program and thank them for working with you. Tell them what you are up to now and that you would like to keep them updated on your progress. You will be amazed at how they respond. Programs are here to help and when you succeed, they all succeed. Remember that.

Getting Along with Work Site Supervisors

There is one thing I want you to remember when you get a new job – *go all out to build a professional relationship with your worksite supervisor.* Make a solid impression, be receptive to what they're telling you, and do the work asked of you – and then some. In your FEO-building years and beyond, there will always be someone higher than you in the chain of command. To better your future and make a difference, getting along with your supervisor is key. And there's no better place to get started learning how to work with your bosses than at your first job.

Think about your experiences with authority – your parents, teachers, the law – and consider how you handled those experiences. It is very likely that how you handle those interactions is how you will handle interactions with your work supervisors. If you have trouble dealing with authority, now is the time to work on it.

There are many reasons why people find dealing with authority a challenge – and most of it is in your brain. People develop what researchers call **control aversion**. Control aversion is a tendency to rebel against control over one's decisions.   It is caused by areas in your brain responsible for attention reorientation and cognitive control. One part of your brain wants to be generous and the other wants to act against any kind of restriction.

Has there ever been a time in your life when you felt that you had control aversion?

To get past control aversion, one must see that no one is really trying to control you They are just trying to get you to do your job. As stated in the previous chapters, your job is not necessarily work. You are a son, daughter, student and some of you are fathers and mothers. Doing your job means living up to your role. People are trying to help you do your job, especially when you fall a little short.

Think of it this way, when you are not stepping up to your role, do you want people to push you further away from your role? Even in situations where you just want people to leave you alone, you must remember no one does it alone. If you feel like people should respect your space and let you fall in a hole, just rate their actions on the survival scale. How would you rate someone who let you learn for yourself? As we said earlier, successful young adults who learn through trial and error will always lose to other young people who learn from others' trial and error.

Don't hate on people who are just trying to give you an up. I have been doing this work for a long time and I never had someone come up to me 20 years later and say, "Mr. Ed, I wished you never pushed me to finish school." Things are about to get real for you and the struggle to maintain a positive attitude and work ethic will be hard. You'll need someone to push you forward, someone to keep you on your toes, so don't push them away.

Get along with your supervisor and allow them to become your mentors, maybe even an OG.

Managing the Boss

Your supervisors' job is to keep you in check. Supervisors are paid to notice if you're just hanging out on your phone or wasting time chatting. They are ten times more stressed out than you because they have to deal with many employees. You only have to deal with one supervisor, maybe two.

Learning how to deal with your supervisor will take time. You must learn about company policies and the personal nuances of the person you're dealing with. The best way to learn how to deal with any supervisor is to ask the people who work with you. In fact, before you take the job, try to build social capital with someone at that workplace so they can give you the rundown on the supervisors and bosses and you can make a good determination if your personalities match. Though, you won't always have the luxury of matching personalities. When a good job comes your way, learn how to handle your business and manage relations. Don't destroy them.

There is nothing wrong with seeking professional help. If you find yourself constantly having conflicts with authority. There are specialists in this area who can walk you through some simple steps to get ahead.

If you have challenges with accomplishing any task, speak to your supervisor about it. You'll be surprised by how accommodating supervisors can be when they know your needs and how to best meet them. Supervisors are there to help you be the best employee you can be – and when you ask them to light the way, you're helping them do their job and helping yourself succeed at the same time.

Understanding Diversity

Now more than ever, we're living in a global culture. As our world grows smaller and more interwoven, it would be a costly mistake to assume you'll only be working alongside people who look, act, or present as you do. Immigration and welcoming people with open arms are cornerstones of the modern world. In your job experience, expect to get to know coworkers whose first language, skin color, sexual orientation, gender expression, and religion differ greatly from yours.

When you are lucky enough to meet someone in your job who is different from you, take a step back and remember not to be rude. Think before asking culturally insensitive questions or making broad assumptions about someone. Before you speak, imagine the script being flipped on you and consider how you would feel if someone said those things to you.

Regardless of where you're coming from, everybody wants to be treated with dignity and respect. Sometimes, that means taking a hard look at your own life and contemplating how to make changes that invite diverse people into your circle. Think about your own group of friends – what demographic is totally unrepresented in the circles you run in? This can be someone's race, gender, religion, body type, sexuality, income, or age.

Instead of holding people at arms' length, when you encounter someone very different from you in your program or job, get to know them! Approach them with an open and kind heart – and no matter what you do, don't ever go up to them and say, "You're (insert personal category here). Tell me about it."

Try asking them about other things: their hobbies, their free time, what brought them to the program, and what they're hoping to get out of it. By bridging cultural gaps, you're not just putting yourself in a position to challenge your own limiting stereotypes and find genuine friendships, but you're eliminating some barriers to social capital.

Think about it: if you're trapped in circles surrounded by your own demographic, it's inevitable that you'll encounter some repetitions in your potential for connections. By branching out and making new friends from all kinds of backgrounds and perspectives, you open yourself up to new levels of opportunity and new chances to foster a diverse social capital framework that can change your life.

Our world's a global one, and chances are you already know and enjoy things that are from a different background than you came from. Whether it's food that you love, a musician you listen to, or a country you've always found interesting, the world is richer when you are open to experiencing the things that the rest of the world has to offer.

Here's a list of simple ways to increase your cultural competence. Let's review the list together. When you're done, I want you to choose one thing that you can work on after completing this course.

- ❖ Seek cultural insight through research, books, and journals.

- ❖ Interact with a diverse group of people

- ❖ Attend diversity training at work

- ❖ Keep building and sharing social capital

Now choose one thing that you can work on after finishing this guide.

_____

_____

Connecting to Opportunity

You never know what someone from a totally different background may have to share that you wouldn't know otherwise. This matters when you consider that it's not just what you know or who you know – it's who you know and who likes you that will determine your success. And nowhere is that more evident than the age divide in our peer groups. There's little to no push on young people to develop relationships with the number one group that can help you develop your future economic opportunity: adults. Expand your social sphere, befriend people different from you including those who are older and be sure to do so with the utmost respect. When you do this, you connect to a large pool of opportunities and that's what building your FEO is all about.

Pronouns

One of the arenas that this respect comes in to play the most is with gender. Gender is an evolving topic in our world and pronouns (the words "he," "she," or "they") matter. The best way to engage with coworkers who are trans or gender non-conforming is by addressing them using the name and pronouns they ask you to use. If you aren't sure about the correct pronouns, ask them one-on-one (avoid big groups because that can put them in potentially life-threatening situations if someone in the group is homophobic or transphobic and violent). A great way to ask is simply, "Hey, (insert name here). What are your preferred pronouns? Mine are…" By sharing your own and asking them theirs, you are showing yourself to be a person they can rely on and trust as a coworker.

Getting Along Effectively with Coworkers

Once you start adopting these attitudes of openness and acceptance, you may find that suddenly you're making friends with your coworkers, no matter what their perspective or background is – and that's great. Sharing a workplace is a healthy and natural cornerstone of many adult friendships, and coworkers who share your interests and motivation can be a pivotal part of helping you grow as a person in the world of work.

It's critical, however, to hold up your professional boundaries with everyone at work. As you get tighter with your coworkers, you may start to backslide on making sure you're as productive at work as you were when you started – and that's something your boss will notice. Think about it. Do you want a potential employer to call your old boss for a reference only to hear them say that you talk way too much on the job? I'm not saying you should ignore your coworkers or avoid making friends. Just be mindful of your productivity and **keep your number one focus where it ought to be: your work.**

This is also important because you never know who's nearby. As you get to know your coworkers and talk with them more and more, stay mindful of the words that come out of your mouth – especially around customers. While it's tempting to get casual and let swearing or personal content filter into your day-to-day talks with coworkers; dishing about parties, romance, or life problems while customers are around isn't exactly setting you up to be employee of the month. Not only could your discussion sell a negative image of the company you work for, but you could also make customers uncomfortable, and get yourself in trouble. Your boss is going to notice sooner or later if you and your coworker are just chilling in the corner or stocking shelves in slow motion in order to talk together longer.

It isn't just your boss who will notice your slow work and distraction, either.

Have you ever been a customer and the employees were just hanging around, talking to each other? It probably didn't make you feel welcome in the store or feel encouraged to come back. In the age of Yelp, Google, and Facebook, it's crucial that you give customers a positive experience. You never know who's going to check in at your workplace and write a stellar (or abysmal) review calling out your customer service skills – or lack thereof. When no customers are around and you're working hard, talking with your coworkers is a wonderful way to brighten up your workplace. There is a way to healthily befriend your coworkers without putting your job at risk. Just remember why you're there – to work – and don't let a conversation, no matter how gripping, steer you away from what you're supposed to be doing.

Boundaries on the Job

Setting boundaries is vital. Without doing this, you invite inappropriate relationships, unprofessional behavior, and habits that can jeopardize your potential to secure references, skills, and future opportunities from your boss.

Bad service and a distracted employee doesn't invite customers to keep shopping. Instead, it sends a message about how little you care. While it may seem more fun to spend time with your friends, text, or hang out, it doesn't help you out in the long run and can make your summer job nothing more than a waste of time.

There's no doubt that boundaries can be difficult to enforce, especially when you're just starting out as an employee. It can be hard to shut down a new friend to go wipe down tables instead, but it pays off in the long run, and your coworker will be motivated by your choices and get their job done too. Drawing the line is important, but it doesn't have to be ice-cold, either.

Try saying something like this, but in your own words, to get you and your coworker back on track: *"I seriously love what we're talking about, but what if we picked it back up after work? I gotta go do X, Y, and Z right now."*

Learning how to deal with all of these challenges will make you ready for workforce success.

Friends Visiting the Job

Of course, keeping on task gets even harder when friends who aren't your coworkers show up at your workplace. When you get a job, the friends you already have may want to come by and see what's up, score a free drink, share their latest escapades, or show you some YouTube videos. As tempting as it is to kick back when your bestie strolls in, it's with these friends who don't work with you that make setting boundaries so important.

If you're chilling with someone who isn't even an employee and you aren't doing your work, your boss is going to question what exactly you're getting paid for, and you could find yourself unemployed, without a reference for the next job, and no better off than you were before.

I'm not here to suggest you should go ahead and give your friends the cold shoulder when they show up. Say "Hi." Be happy to see them – but set boundaries for yourself.

One simple and noninflammatory way to acknowledge your friend while letting them know you have to get moving is by saying something along the lines of, *"I gotta get back to work, but I'll hit you up once I'm off the clock!"*

This lets them know that you need to get back to work and signals that you have tasks on your plate while showing you value their time and friendship. After all, your future economic opportunities are on the line, and if the friend you're hanging with is worth holding onto, they'll respect the boundaries you set and be happy to see you're putting your future first.

Relationships at Work

Romance is a wonderful thing. When love is in the air, it can feel like the world is your oyster. Especially when you're younger, it can feel like love is around just about every other corner. But there's a time and a place to prioritize romance – and it isn't while you're on the clock. While you're working, you'll be spending a lot of time with your coworkers. You may even think a couple of them are cute. But above all other things – avoid romance with your coworkers. Flirting isn't on the table while you're at work. Not only will your boss notice your distraction, but you may also be making your coworker uncomfortable without realizing it. Maybe the person you're working with hasn't read this book and doesn't know the tips you have for setting boundaries. Maybe they're afraid that if they turn you down, you'll make it hard to work with them. Maybe they're afraid of starting drama by friend-zoning you.

The best thing to do? Avoid putting your coworkers in a bad situation in the first place. Be polite; don't say anything to a coworker you wouldn't be comfortable saying in front of your mom (or your boss, for that matter). To steer clear of putting someone in a situation that makes working miserable, just don't comment on their appearance, positively or negatively, and never ask them on a date. Things like this make for a sour work environment that can land you in a world of trouble. Thanks to the #MeToo movement, many people are finding their voices and standing up to situations that make them uncomfortable, and more bosses are feeling the pressure to hold their colleagues accountable. If you haven't done so before, search #MeToo on Twitter or Instagram. Read up on the culture and be part of the solution.

These boundaries don't stop at your coworkers. When interacting with customers, there's an even bigger necessity for all interactions to be professional, not an opportunity to make new friends. Customers show up at your workplace to get their coffee or groceries, or to receive a service. They're not coming to the restaurant on the prowl for a love connection. Flirting with a customer can make them uncomfortable. When you flirt with a customer you risk them, at best, never coming back and your actions costing the company a customer. At worst, the customer can choose to report you to your boss, putting your job and FEO on the line.

Even if you're 99% sure the feeling is mutual, still greet the situation with professionalism and put your job first. If your gut is right and the other person feels the same way, then your drive and dedication to your job will only help you. What's more impressive than being motivated to succeed?

SAFETY

Above all other things, make sure you're exercising safety as you head out into the working world, both with who you spend time with after work, and the job tasks themselves.

Nowadays, many protections are in place to help you stay safe on the job. If you're under eighteen, it can be frustrating to not be allowed to operate heavy machinery, baking, or deli equipment, but learning the other jobs in the field is a great first step to learning the ropes. You'll have the rest of your life to operate the equipment. For now, master the work you're allowed to, and you'll be more than equipped to learn how to use the machinery down the line.

More than that, be wary when you interact with people. Use your instincts. Adults often do have your best interests in mind, but some people will take advantage of you. If an adult sets off any alarm bells in your head, listen to the alarms.

An adult, supervisor, coworker, or customer should never say something or ask you to do something that makes you feel unsafe. If something does happen, it's their fault, but take preventative steps when possible: don't go places with adults that you don't know and that aren't part of your program. Only spend time with the adults who run the program in approved settings and never meet them at their home or somewhere you'll be alone. And remember: if an adult is acting suspiciously, harassing you, or making you otherwise uncomfortable, remember that it is most likely not you are misinterpreting a situation. Speak up, don't let adults walk all over you, and always put your safety first.

When you're communicating, connecting, and building up your FEO wisely, you'll be ready for workforce success and beyond.

OGs Shared Knowledge

In this chapter, I learned about how best to conduct myself while on the job. I spoke about it with my OG _____.

We discussed:

_____

_____

_____

They suggested:

_____

_____

_____

I also talked to them about ways that I can improve at work. They advised:

_____

_____

I will apply this advice to my life at work by:

_____

_____

_____

I'll be sure to keep them updated on my progress every _____.

Date completed: _____

CHAPTER 10

In the streets, we know the importance of surrounding yourself with people who have your back. But what does that mean? All too often, "having your back" translates to someone who will do dirt with you and help you ultimately lose your life, freedom, or future economic opportunity.

What if having someone's back meant the opposite? What would it look like if the people who had your back were there to do whatever it takes to break, shake, forsake any downward spin? What if they were there to help you begin again - to support you in your journey towards life, freedom, and future economic opportunity. Wouldn't that be a great day?

Here at the MAKiN iT Nation, we urge you to never give up till you find yourselves surrounded by those types of people. Always remember: **a true friend will never lead you to danger.**

In the workplace, you want to surround yourself with similar types of people. Leaders who are willing to push you towards excellence and vouch for you when you need it. When two equally qualified candidates reach for the same opportunity, it's always the one with the personal connection that lands that job. This is even more crucial when you find yourself up against applicants who are even more qualified than you. To get your first big break, you need to overwhelm the hiring manager with several credible people who are willing to vouch for your skills, motivation, and ability to work hard.

So how do you get others to vouch for you? First, avoid these vouch killers from day one:

1. **Being consistently late**

   By being consistently late, you are sending a message to your coworkers and supervisors that you don't care about their time so why should they take time out of their day to care about yours?

2. **Having a stink face or salty attitude**

   That may just be your demeanor but realize the message that you are sending to others. Most importantly think about why you have that face and make every effort to smile as much as possible no matter how you are feeling.

3. **Not completing your task**

   No one wants to do your work just like you don't want to do other peoples' work. If you don't know how to get something done, speak to your supervisor.

4. **Texting on the job**

   Under no circumstances should you send or read texts unless they are work-related. Your boyfriend texting you about what time he is going to pick you up is not work-related.

5. **Giving bad customer service**

   If you drive customers away, your boss will drive you away. Don't think that bad interaction will go unnoticed. In this virtual age, a customer will write a bad review quicker than you can tie your shoes and they will blast it out to the whole world to see. It will not only impact your job but every job that you plan to get in the future.

6. **Never taking the time to learn or do more work**

   The world is yours and Brother Yo-UTU-Be is here to help you prepare for it. Remember his government name is YOUTUBE. This is no excuse not to learn. Everything you need is at your fingertips and there are people always there to help.

If you work hard, you'll make many valuable connections and lay the groundwork for future references.

References

It can be scary to reach out to a coworker or supervisor, especially when we think that we have nothing to offer. But you do have something to offer. It's something that the majority of other workers don't offer – you put in work. Remember, out of an 8-hour workday, the average employee only puts in three hours of hard work. We looked at this in chapter 8. Just remember this when the time comes for you to reach out for a reference. You are a hard worker and people want to help those who work hard.

Let's look at a way to ask someone to be a reference. You may want to say something like, *"Mary, I enjoy working with you. I'm thinking of applying to school one day and I wanted to ask you if it's ok for me to use you as a reference?"* Wait for an answer then add if appropriate, *"If it's ok, I can send you a sample reference letter that you can edit."* If you are a hard worker, Mary will say yes. The trick will be getting Mary to write the reference letter. Most people don't like writing, or they don't have the time for it. That's a fact.   That's why we offered to write the reference letter for Mary and invited Mary to edit it as they see fit. That way you will ensure it gets done.

Here is a sample reference letter:

> **I am enthusiastic to recommend Carlos. I have known Carlos for 8 months. Carlos has always displayed a high degree of responsibility, respect, and quality customer service. While working at Everyday Office Solutions, Carlos always made others smile. In addition to Carlos' accomplishments as a customer service representative, Carlos has proven his leadership abilities by implementing a new customer feedback protocol. Moreover, Carlos is a dependable team player – like the time he worked two 8-hour shifts for two weeks to cover a sick co-worker. Carlos has a great personality, a mature sense of self, and he is always eager to learn. It is my firm belief that Carlos would be a remarkable asset to any organization, and I am happy to give Carlos my recommendation.**
>
> **Sincerely,**

Remember, getting a reference is easy. All you have to do is 1) be prepared to ask for reference and 2) give the person assistance in getting the reference letter done.

Let's try it out.

Speak to two of your OGs and ask them for a reference letter. Use the reference letter script as well as the written sample to get it done. Keep your chin up, your shoulders back, and go out there and get at least two reference letters. You may even use the letters when applying for your next job.

The Credibility You Need

Although jobs end, your social capital doesn't. So how do you continue to build social capital with your former supervisor and others once the job is done? You must stay connected! While most people know that follow-up is important, very few do it.

Did you know that the majority of sales are made on the 8th contact and that most salespeople give up after the second try? Think about all those lost sales. Leaving a voicemail or sending an e-mail is not a follow-up. Your future career success will be based on who you know just as much as what you know. Forgetting to stay in contact with those who helped you is economic suicide. Staying in contact is not about nagging or harassing. It's about reminding. Remind them of the wonderful, valuable ways that they contributed to your growth and development and show them the fruits of their efforts.

Let me put it like this, ***staying connected is all about acknowledgment.*** People like to be acknowledged. Social capital builders and Opportunity Seekers know that recognizing others is a major part of the social capital building process and the easiest. It is all about giving. As we discussed earlier, social capital is not about receiving, it's about giving. Opportunity Seekers know that staying connected and updating people on your progress is a wonderful way to give and much, much easier than trying to reconnect.

What do you think credibility means? I like to define credibility as the believability of a source or message. **Credibility is a person's assessment of your believability**. To put it simply, they will do things for you if they believe in you. It's your job to make them believe.

Use every accomplishment you make as an opportunity to establish and build your credibility! Take advantage of every one of those achievements, no matter how small, by communicating them to your former supervisors or bosses. Start today by updating them on your progress in this Workforce and Summer Job Success guide. As an Opportunity Seeker, an official member of the MAKiN' iT Nation, you should know that the best way to establish credibility is by demonstrating your commitment to your FEO. We call these FEO commitments.

You will build credibility with every adult by showcasing your FEO accomplishments. To do this, you should focus on:

1. **Telling**—Make adults believe and trust what you say. Tell them what active steps you took since leaving the job or school to build your future economic opportunities. This gives your message credibility, plus people always like to hear the steps young people are taking to improve their lives.

2. **Showing**—Back up your statements with compelling evidence. Give your former supervisor convincing evidence that you are making progress in your FEO (certificates, degrees, enrollment letters, photographs, videos, etc.). For example, if you want to convince a former supervisor that you have been pursuing your education, send them a copy of your most recent progress report. If you have been looking for work, mention that you are following the Workforce and Summer Job Success guide and that you would like for them to serve as one of your Opportunity Guides (OGs).

3. **Calling**—Call on others to back up your claims. You would be surprised by the power of a second-party source. Similar to the reference letter activity earlier, having someone to back up your claim is a powerful tool to establish credibility. It's simple to ask a teacher or community leader to write a blurb about your character and/or performance. As you ask, you will be building more social capital in the process.

4. **Admitting**—Be honest about your setbacks and be prepared to show your former supervisor and others how you corrected yourself. People trust people who admit mistakes. Everyone makes them. When people don't admit to mistakes, people know they are not telling the truth.

Writing letters, sending emails, scheduling visits, and phone calls are only a few of the ways that you can and should stay connected with your social capital assets. As Social Capital Builders, we have developed an entire framework to keep young people connected to the people and places where most opportunities are born. Never forget that it is up to you to keep those connections and foster those relationships to bring about your success.

CONGRATULATIONS!

You've worked your way through job success and now you are finally ready to go out there and get it! Remember, your future economic opportunity will always be dependent on who you connect with and how well you cherish those connections. Those connections are meant to help you grow as a person and an employee. To help you continue your social capital building, fill out the chart below with your OGs and connects name, info, and how often you will reach out to them. You got this! Good luck!

Name	Contact Info	Frequency

Name	Contact Info	Frequency